SEMINAR EDITIONS

SEMINAR EDITIONS

Theodore G. Tappert, General Editor

PIA DESIDERIA

by PHILIP JACOB SPENER

Translated, edited, and with an Introduction by
THEODORE G. TAPPERT

FORTRESS PRESS · PHILADELPHIA

© 1964 BY FORTRESS PRESS

2nd printing, 1967

Library of Congress Catalog Card Number 64-12995

5846E67   Printed in U. S. A.   1-1953

SEMINAR EDITIONS

Christian literature of the past, when read and pondered after the lapse of generations, often sheds new light on the discussion of important questions in our day. Revival of interest in the writings of such diverse figures of the past as Søren Kierkegaard, Blaise Pascal, John Wesley, John Calvin, Martin Luther, Thomas Aquinas, and Augustine (to mention only a few) has served such a function.

Acquaintance with the literature of the past also provides first-hand glimpses into the life and thought of Christians in earlier ages. Men whose names have been encountered in history text-books take on flesh and blood, and important movements in the history of the church come into clearer focus when the literary deposit of other times is read.

It is the purpose of the present series to make available to the modern reader a number of works which deserve to be better known. Most of them are here translated into English for the first time; the few which were originally written in English have long been out of print. All have been edited with care and furnished with introductions and annotations which will help the reader understand them in their historical context.

The choice of various types of literature—diaries, memoirs, and correspondence as well as theological essays—should add interest to instruction for the general reader as well as the student of church history and the history of Christian thought. The same may be said for the inclusion of European as well as American works.

47476

CONTENTS

Introduction: the Times, the Man, the Book   1

The Text of the *Pia Desideria*   29

  Salutation and Circumstances of Writing   30

  Conspectus of Corrupt Conditions in the Church   39
    Defects in Civil Authorities   43
    Defects in the Clergy   44
    Defects in the Common People   57
    Offenses Resulting from these Defects   68

  The Possibility of Better Conditions in the Church   76

  Proposals to Correct Conditions in the Church   87
    More Extensive Use of the Scriptures   87
    Exercise of the Spiritual Priesthood   92
    Practice vs. Knowledge of Christianity   95
    Conduct of Religious Controversies   97
    Reform of Schools and Universities   103
    Preaching for Purposes of Edification   115

Table of Contents of the Appendixes   123

Index   127

INTRODUCTION

During the seventeenth and eighteenth centuries Christendom experienced a revival of moral and religious earnestness. The revival did not appear everywhere at the same time, nor did it always assume precisely the same form. Negatively it represented a protest against the formalism in doctrine, worship, and life into which churches and their members had fallen after the original impulses of the Reformation had dissipated. Positively it represented an attempt to cultivate a keener awareness of the present reality of God's judgment and grace and the bearing which these were believed to have on personal and social life. We can observe evidences of all this not only in the English Puritanism of the late sixteenth and early seventeenth centuries and in the Pietism of the European continent during the late seventeenth and early eighteenth centuries, but also in the contemporary Jansenist movement within Roman Catholicism and the Hasidist movement in Judaism. The English Puritan John Bunyan, the Dutch Reformed Willem Teelinck, the German Lutheran Philip Jacob Spener, the Moravian Nicholas Zinzendorf, the Methodist progenitor John Wesley, the American Presbyterian Gilbert Tennent, and the Roman Catholic Blaise Pascal—all of these were participants in a common historical climate although they reacted differently in their concrete historical situations.[1]

[1] An excellent brief analysis of Puritanism, Pietism, and Evangelicalism is available in John T. McNeill, *Modern Christian Movements* (Philadelphia: Westminster Press, 1954), pp. 15-103. On the likenesses and differences between Puritanism and Pietism see pp. 71-74.

Both the common climate and a concrete situation are reflected in what Richard Baxter recorded in his *Autobiography* of the criticism he heard as a boy, in 1630, about his Anglican father:

When I heard them speak scornfully of others as Puritans whom I never knew, I was at first apt to believe all the Lies and Slanders wherewith they loaded them. But when I heard my own Father so reproached and perceived the Drunkards were the forwardest in the reproach, I perceived that it was mere Malice. For my Father never scrupled Common Prayer or Ceremonies, nor spake against Bishops, nor ever so much as prayed but by a Book or Form, being not ever acquainted then with any who did otherwise. But only for reading Scripture when the rest were Dancing on the Lord's Day, and for praying (by a Form out of the end of the Common Prayer Book) in his House, and for reproving Drunkards and Swearers, and for talking sometimes a few words of Scripture and the Life to come, he was reviled commonly by the name of Puritan, Precisian and Hypocrite: and so were the godly conformable Ministers that lived everywhere in the country near us, not only by our neighbors, but by the common talk of the Vulgar Rabble all around us. [2]

Here was an attempt, within the framework of a particular religious tradition, to take the Christian life seriously in a way that evoked opposition and ridicule. Richard Baxter's father was in his own way a reformer in the Church of England. Philip Jacob Spener was a reformer in the Lutheran church in Germany.

1

In order to understand Spener's reform it is necessary to inquire what the situation was like when and where he lived and labored.[3] At the close of the Thirty Years' War in 1648 Germany was di-

[2] Richard Baxter, *Reliquiae Baxterianae, or Mr. Richard Baxter's Narrative of the Most Memorable Passages of his Life and Times*, 1696 ed., pp. 2, 3. I owe this quotation from Baxter's autobiography to Hugh Martin, *Puritanism and Richard Baxter* (London: S.C.M. Press, 1954).

[3] For a fuller bibliography see T. G. Tappert, "Orthodoxism, Pietism, and Rationalism: 1580-1830," in *Christian Social Responsibility*, ed. Harold C. Letts (3 vols., Philadelphia: Muhlenberg Press, 1957), II, 36-88.

vided into more than three hundred territories or states, each of which was governed by a prince or other ruler. As was the case at the time in other European countries, these rulers claimed that their power was absolute because it was received directly from God and owed nothing to the consent of the people. A rather typical contemporaneous statement of the relation of the ruler and the people declared:

> Even if a ruler is godless, tyrannical, and greedy, it is nevertheless not proper for his subjects to resist or oppose such godlessness, tyranny, and greed but rather to acknowledge these as the chastisements of the Almighty which the subjects have by their sins deserved. Accordingly it is not proper for subjects to demand new statutes, for it is the office of the ruler to make laws, and subjects are under obligation to render due obedience to their rulers. [4]

The absolutist pretensions of the rulers inevitably affected the church. In the sixteenth century the Reformers had turned to the German princes, as "the chief members of the church,"[5] to take a hand in the reform of the church in their lands. This appeal for provisional assistance had led in time to a condition of permanent control. By the second half of the seventeenth century many of the rulers were members of the church only in a nominal sense, yet they held ecclesiastical legislation and appointments firmly in their grasp. Other rulers, who continued to be sincere in their Christian profession and had good intentions, meddled in the inner life of the church to its serious detriment. Church and state were united in such a way that the state controlled the church, and the ministers of the church became officials of the state.

Generally a ruler exercised his control over the church through a consistory, which was a standing commission composed of clergy-

[4] Quoted in Friedrich Uhlhorn, *Geschichte der deutsch-lutherischen Kirche* (2 vols., Leipzig: Dörffling & Franke, 1911), I, 198.
[5] Philip Melanchthon, "Treatise on the Power and Primacy of the Pope" (1537), sec. 54, in *The Book of Concord*, trans. and ed. T. G. Tappert *et al.* (Philadelphia: Muhlenberg Press, 1959), p. 329.

men and lawyers appointed by and responsible to the ruler. In the course of the seventeenth century such consistories came to be dominated by bureaucratic lawyers, and sometimes these men had interest in the church only as a legal institution. Subject to the direction of the consistories were superintendents, who had oversight over all the churches and the ministers in a district. In some respects they exercised episcopal functions—and, in fact, the title "superintendent" was from an old Latin variant of the Greek word for "bishop." In imperial free cities the pattern was as a rule similar to that in principalities or kingdoms. The town council or senate appointed a consistory or other board, and the body of clergymen (*ministerium*), presided over by a senior (*senior ministerii*), was permitted to do no more than make recommendations to the consistory or to the senate. Whether in free cities or in principalities, congregations had no independent powers beyond the right to object to a minister who was sent to serve them. As the territorial church was subject to the lordship of the ruler, transmitted through consistory and superintendent, the congregation was subject to the rule of its minister, who often acted more like a policeman than a pastor.

Although it was still customary in the seventeenth century for German princes to have court chaplains, the influence of such chaplains was on the wane. As a rule they became as obsequious toward their rulers as other courtiers, and they distinguished themselves more by their flattery than by their candor. As far as the princes themselves are concerned, some were able and upright, others were irresponsible, and still others managed to unite diligence in prayer with almost unbelievable wantonness. Class distinctions were rigidly observed, and so the princes and the rest of the nobility not only expected but actually received outward marks of respect and devotion from all the other people. Under the nobility were professional people, notably lawyers and clergymen, and rich burghers. At the bottom of the scale were the workers and peasants. Such class distinctions were manifest in the churches, where elevated and upholstered places were reserved for the upper classes and only the common people sat on hard seats in the nave. Besides, the upper classes often insisted on having their baptisms, weddings, funerals, and communions in private (whether in the church or at home), and so it was only for the common people that such acts continued to be performed in the church.

Ecclesiastical distinctions were as sharply drawn as class distinctions. Absolutist rulers saw political advantage in religious uniformity within their territories and were intolerant toward confessions other than their own. Protestant sentiment against Roman Catholicism was exceeded only by controversy within Protestantism. The expansion of the Reformed at the close of the sixteenth and beginning of the seventeenth centuries into territories (like Anhalt, Baden, Hessen, Brandenburg) which had previously been Lutheran evoked bitter resentment. This was expressed in sarcastic lampoons of each other's teachings and practice—all the more merciless because Lutherans and Reformed were actually the closest theological relatives.[6] Attempts were made to achieve at least a measure of understanding in a series of colloquies between Lutheran and Roman Catholic and between Lutheran and Reformed theologians, but little came of them. Religious intolerance may be said to be the hallmark of the seventeenth century, but there were instances (especially in southwestern Germany) of Lutheran sponsors at Reformed baptisms and Reformed communicants at Lutheran altars.

Interconfessional polemics occupied a prominent place in the education of ministers. Latin was still the medium for theological instruction in the universities. Emphasis was placed on inculcat-

---

[6] The title of a series of theses by the Wittenberg professor Polycarp Leyser was "Whether, How, and Why one Should Have Fellowship with and Place Confidence in the Papists rather than with and in the Calvinists" (1602). It was customary at this time to call Lutherans "Evangelicals," as in the locution "the Evangelical and the Reformed theologians." Spener so used the term in his *Pia Desideria.*

ing by rote the contents of an inherited theology, reduced to a compendium[7] and expounded with reference to current controversies. The philosophy of Aristotle played a large part in the formulation of the church's teaching and in the public disputations by means of which students were trained to argue in defense of the theology they were taught. The treatment of ethics rested on Aristotle or, in its more relevant form, was casuistical. Independent exegesis of the Scriptures had little place in the curriculum at a time when it was assumed that the contents of the Scriptures were adequately expressed in the Confessions. The want of a historical understanding of the past, even of the Reformation, contributed to the tendency to look upon theological statements as timeless truths and to identify the Christian faith with intellectual propositions.

The dominant emphasis on an intellectually formulated and exclusively delimited "pure teaching" was accompanied by other, although for the time being more subdued, currents. The great systematic theologian John Gerhard (1582-1637) accommodated himself to the prevailing orthodoxism, complained privately in his correspondence about the need for reform, and cultivated a mystical religion which was borrowed from the late Middle Ages and was expressed in his *Sacred Meditations*.[8] Balthasar Meisner (1587-1626), professor in Wittenberg and an unrelenting contender against Calvinism, lectured about the shortcomings of the clergy and civil rulers in the society of his day and proposed improvements. The versatile John Valentine Andreae (1586-1643) criticized the contentiousness of theologians, the interference of princes in the affairs of the church, and the religious illiteracy of the people while he engaged actively in social reform. Theophilus Gross-

[7] For an English translation of a favorite see Leonard Hutter, *A Compend of Lutheran Theology* (1610), translated from the Latin by H. E. Jacobs and G. F. Spieker (Philadelphia: Lutheran Book Store, 1873).

[8] John Gerhard, *Sacred Meditations,* translated from the Latin by C. W. Heisler (Philadelphia, 1896).

gebauer (1626-1661) deplored the supplanting of constructive pastoral work by preoccupation with theological polemics. For the most part these were voices crying in the wilderness.

Ministers who were trained in Latin must have experienced great difficulties in translating their theology into the language of the people, and contemporary complaints about the insertion in sermons of quotations in foreign tongues would seem to bear this out. Ministers whose training centered so largely in disputations and polemics must have encountered trouble in edifying their parishioners, and contemporary criticisms seem to support this. Ministers who lived in a time when society was sharply divided into classes must have run into many serious obstacles, and contemporary complaints that they were too servile and fawning before princes and noblemen and that they lorded it over the common people are not surprising in the circumstances. Nor is it altogether surprising to discover that many ministers shared the current belief in witchcraft and succumbed to the current vices of the people, including excesses in food and drink.

Yet most of the people, even in the cities, were regular in their attendance of Sunday services. That they were not always attentive is suggested by regulations which prohibited walking to and fro and gossiping during prayers and hymns. Sleeping during sermons, which were not only long but often beyond the comprehension of the auditors, was so common that the distinguished theologian John Gerhard was expressly praised at his funeral for never having slept in church.[9] People attended church partly because they were required to do so by law, and attendance was sometimes thought of as a good work whose mere performance gave them credit in God's sight. Even more was participation in the Lord's Supper regarded as an act which had a mechanical effect on one's relation to God, and most people were regular communicants,

[9] Paul Grünberg, *Philipp Jakob Spener* (3 vols., Göttingen, 1893-1906), I, 27.

7

whether once a year, once a quarter, or (occasionally) once a month. In spite of the outwardly flourishing condition of the church, there seemed to be little evidence of genuine Christian life. At least, this was the complaint that was widely heard long before Philip Jacob Spener was born.

2

It was in the Alsatian village of Rappoltstein, not far from Strasbourg, that Philip Jacob Spener was born on January 13, 1635.[10] His father was a steward and later a councilor of one of the dukes of Rappoltstein. To his mother, he later testified, he was especially indebted for his early religious impulses. One of the sponsors at his baptism, a woman of the house of Rappoltstein, also had a formative influence on him when he was a boy. Even greater, however, was the influence which his pastor Joachim Stoll (1615-1678) had on the young man as catechist, preacher, and counselor. This man later married Spener's oldest sister, remained his respected adviser, and wrote the second appendix to his *Pia Desideria*.

An omnivorous reader from his youth, Spener's early years were also shaped by books which he found in his father's library. Next to the Bible his favorite was John Arndt's *True Christianity*, a devotional book which later became as popular in the Scandinavian countries as in Germany and was carried to America by many colonists. John Arndt (1555-1621) had asserted that orthodox doctrine was not enough to produce Christian life and advocated a mysticism which he borrowed largely from the late Middle Ages.

---

[10] For the life of Spener see especially Grünberg, *op. cit.*, I, 125-381. A popular biography is Hans Bruns, *Ein Reformator nach der Reformation: Leben und Wirken P. J. Speners* (Marburg: Spener-Verlag, 1937). In English there is only a brief and unsatisfactory sketch in M. E. Richard, *P. J. Spener and his Work* (Philadelphia: Lutheran Publication Society, 1897), and a fictionalized life by Karl A. Wildenhahn, *Philip Jacob Spener* (Philadelphia: J. F. Smith, 1881).

Toward the close of his life he explained why he wrote *True Christianity*, which was originally published between 1606 and 1609:

> In the first place, I wished to withdraw the minds of students and preachers from an inordinately controversial and polemical theology which has well-nigh assumed the form of an earlier scholastic theology. Secondly, I purposed to conduct Christian believers from lifeless thoughts to such as might bring forth fruit. Thirdly, I wished to guide them onward from mere science and theory to the actual practice of faith and godliness. And fourthly, to show them wherein a truly Christian life that accords with true faith consists, as well as to explain the apostle's meaning when he says, "I live; yet not I, but Christ liveth in me," etc. (Gal. 2:30).[11]

In his boyhood Spener also read several English books which he found in German translation in his father's library and which had for some time enjoyed a wide circulation on the continent. One was Emanuel Sontham's *Golden Treasure of the Children of God*[12] and another was Lewis Bayly's *The Practice of Piety* (1610?). These were supplemented by later reading in Daniel Dyke's *Nosce te ipsum, or Self-deceit* (1614) and Richard Baxter's *The Necessary Teaching of the Denial of Self* (*ca.* 1650). All these devotional books by English Puritans were critical of conventional Christianity. They advocated self-examination, an earnest quest for holiness, and otherworldly standards of morality which would set the true Christian apart from his neighbor. They shared with John Arndt an emphasis on a rigorous religious and moral life as over against a dogmatic intellectualism, but they were less mystical. The influence of such books, as well as of persons who helped shape Spener's youth, is suggested in the answer which he later gave to Baron von Canstein's question, whether he had in his early

[11] John Arndt, *True Christianity*, trans. and ed. A. W. Boehm and Charles F. Schaeffer (Philadelphia: Smith, English & Co., 1868), p. xxxi.

[12] John T. McNeill, *op. cit.*, p. 53, conjectures that this was translated from an unpublished English manuscript.

years been a bad boy: "Indeed, I was bad, for I remember very well that when I was twelve years old I saw some people dance and was persuaded by others to join in the dancing. Hardly had I begun, however, when I was overtaken by such fear that I ran away from the dance and never since that time tried it again."[13]

At the age of sixteen, after completing his preparatory studies, Spener was matriculated in the University of Strasbourg. There he devoted his time especially to the study of philosophy, history, and languages. Within two years he was granted a master's degree, and he served as instructor in history during his subsequent study of theology. The professor of theology who influenced him most, according to Spener's later statements, was John Conrad Dannhauer (1603-1666). It was he who induced Spener to read Luther's works. It was he who first taught Spener to think of salvation as a present and not merely a future gift of God. It was he who opened Spener's eyes to the place of the laity in the church. It was he who suggested the use of the vernacular instead of Latin in some phases of theological education. It was from him that Spener learned the casuistical treatment of ethics, and to him that Spener appealed for support in his views on Sunday observance. This is not to suggest that there were no differences between the two men, for Dannhauer was a representative of the scholastic tradition of seventeenth-century theology in a way in which Spener was not.

As a student in Strasbourg Spener lived a rather ascetic and secluded life. He did not participate in the drinking bouts, the fencing matches, or the dancing which occupied the attention of other students. He avoided members of the opposite sex and had few friends of his own. One day a week he did not eat dinner, perhaps following a suggestion concerning fasting in Bayly's *Practice*

[13] Carl Hildebrand von Canstein, *Ausführliche Beschreibung der Lebens-Geschichte . . . des seligen Herrn D. Philipp Jakob Speners*, in *Speners Kleine Geistliche Schriften*, ed. J. A. Steinmetz (2 vols., Magdeburg, 1741), I, 16.

10

of Piety, until he was compelled to give this up for reasons of health. In keeping with the advice of his future brother-in-law Joachim Stoll, he refrained from theological study as well as worldly pleasure on Sundays; he spent the day, after attending church, in reading and discussing devotional literature with a few friends.

After he completed his theological studies in the summer of the year 1659, Spener spent two years in travel. This was customary at the time. In Spener's case these years of travel were more than ordinarily significant. He spent varying lengths of time in Basel, Bern, Lausanne, and Geneva in Switzerland, Lyons and Montbéliard in France, and Freiburg and Tübingen in Germany. In Geneva he became acquainted with the zealous French Reformed preacher Jean de Labadie (1610-1674) when he was at the height of his influence and before he lapsed into his later mystical fanaticism. The very fact that Spener often went to hear him indicates something of the impression Labadie made on his young visitor. The fact that Spener had one of Labadie's French tracts published in a German translation[14] about six years later suggests that the impression remained. Travel to cities in foreign countries also gave Spener an opportunity to become better acquainted with Reformed church life, and especially to observe the organizational patterns developed among the French-speaking Reformed.

When Spener returned to Strasbourg at the conclusion of his travels he did some teaching, he was ordained as a stated assistant preacher, he wrote a dissertation for the degree of doctor of theology, and he was married to a twenty-year-old girl recommended by his mother—all within a period of two years. Although Spener had been preparing himself with a view to teaching, he was diverted from this goal by a call he received in the spring of 1666 to serve as senior of the clergy in Frankfurt am Main. Moved by

[14] *Kurzer Unterricht von andächtiger Betrachtung* (Frankfurt, 1667). See Grünberg, *op. cit.,* I, 170; III, 253.

a sense of duty rather than by any confidence in his own fitness, he accepted and moved to the prominent center of trade and culture in western Germany. His duties as *senior ministerii* included preaching and administering the sacraments at the early service in the city's principal church, presiding over meetings of the city's twelve or more ministers, ordaining or installing new ministers, visiting parishes, and keeping records of pastoral acts, etc. Although only thirty-one years old and placed above colleagues who were twice his age, he set about his work with a vigor which was remarkable in a man of his reserved and timid nature.

He began at once to strengthen the program for instructing children in the catechism on Sunday afternoons (*Kinderlehre*) and made some tentative efforts to revive the rite of confirmation. He urged the civil authorities in Frankfurt to enact and enforce legislation to curb ostentatious attire and forbid trade on Sunday, but with little success. He began to carry on an extensive correspondence, especially with members of the nobility, through which he became in time what somebody has called "the spiritual counselor of all Germany." During these years, moreover, Spener became acquainted, personally or otherwise, with several men who were trying to put an end to the current religious intolerance. One of these was John Dury (1596-1689),[15] a native of Scotland who spent half a century on the continent in an attempt to reconcile the Reformed and the Lutherans. Spener once declared that he saw more evidence of true Christian discipleship in Dury than in many of his own Lutheran brethren, but he regarded the Scotsman's efforts as unrealistic. A second was the young philosopher Gottfried Wilhelm Leibniz (1646-1716), who lived in Frankfurt for a while during Spener's early years there. The two became personal friends and later corresponded on literary and historical topics as well as on the subject of church union, which was a concern of Leibniz.

[15] Cf. J. M. Batten, *John Dury, Advocate of Christian Reunion* (Chicago: University of Chicago Press, 1944).

Finally, he became involved in the proposal for church union which had been advanced by the theologian George Calixtus (1586-1656) when Duke Ernest of Gotha requested a formal opinion. Calixtus recommended that the churches unite by returning to the consensus of the first five centuries of the Christian era. Spener seemed not to recognize that, apart from placing tradition above the Scriptures, this proposal made an unhistorical use of history. In fact, although he expressed some sympathy for the intention of Calixtus, he remained noncommittal and evasive.

More important in Spener's career in Frankfurt was his encouragement of lay religion. In a sermon which he preached in 1669 Spener declared:

> How much good it would do if good friends would come together on a Sunday and instead of getting out glasses, cards, or dice would take up a book and read from it for the edification of all or would review something from sermons that were heard! If they would speak with one another about the divine mysteries, and the one who received most from God would try to instruct his weaker brethren! If, should they be not quite able to find their way through, they would ask a preacher to clarify the matter! If this should happen, how much evil would be held in abeyance, and how the blessed Sunday would be sanctified for the great edification and marked benefit of all! It is certain, in any case, that we preachers cannot instruct the people from our pulpits as much as is needful unless other persons in the congregation, who by God's grace have a superior knowledge of Christianity, take the pains, by virtue of their universal Christian priesthood, to work with and under us to correct and reform as much in their neighbors as they are able according to the measure of their gifts and their simplicity. [16]

This is the earliest known reference which Spener made to the holding of private meetings for the cultivation of holiness, the so-called *collegia pietatis*. Attempts have been made to show the de-

---

[16] Spener, *Erbauliche Evangelisch- und Epistolische Sonntags-Andachten* (Frankfurt, 1716), p. 638, quoted in Grünberg, *op. cit.*, I, 165.

pendence of these on the house meetings of Jean de Labadie in Geneva, the "prophesyings" of the Puritans in England, or similar assemblies among the Reformed in the Netherlands and among Lutherans in various parts of Germany. There is no evidence to prove such dependence. The most that can be said with assurance is that the *collegia pietatis* were not out of keeping with the character of Spener's whole previous experience and piety and that they reflected the common historical climate which produced similar phenomena elsewhere.

It was not until the following year, 1670, that the first private meeting for edification under Spener's leadership actually came into being at the request of a few parishioners. The meetings were held Sundays and Wednesdays in Spener's home. Both men and women attended, seated separately from each other, and only the men were permitted to speak. Meetings were opened with prayer. The sermon of the previous Sunday was discussed, or else passages were read from a devotional book (Joachim Luetkemann's *Vorschmack der göttlichen Güte*[17] and Lewis Bayly's *Practice of Piety* were used) and made the basis for edifying conversation. Later on passages of the Bible were made the center of discussion. Some of Spener's fellow ministers in Frankfurt attended these meetings but for the most part remained rather reserved in their judgment.

3

Spener was a prolific writer,[18] as we shall have more occasion to note, but the writing that first called him to the attention of his contemporaries and on which his fame especially rests is his *Pia Desideria*. A Frankfurt publisher planned to put out a new

---

[17] "Foretaste of Divine Goodness" (Wolfenbüttel, 1643). Lütkemann represented the same tradition as John Arndt, and like Arndt he was a forerunner of Spener.

[18] Grünberg, *op. cit.*, III, 213-264, lists about 300 published items, including sermons, devotional tracts, prefaces to books by others, catechetical literature, polemical works, books on history, genealogy, and heraldry, correspondence, etc.

edition of John Arndt's perennially popular sermons on the appointed Gospels of the church year (originally published in 1615) in time for the spring book fair. He asked Spener to write a new preface for this edition, and Spener used the occasion to set down some things about which he had long been reflecting. In keeping with his customary caution he discussed the contents of the preface with his fellow ministers in Frankfurt and secured their encouragement before he submitted his manuscript. The preface created such an immediate sensation that the author had it published separately within six months, furnished with a title of its own, introduced with a dedication "to all officials and pastors," and followed by extended comments (appendixes) requested from two friends. In this form, comprising 344 pages duodecimo, it appeared in the fall of 1675. Another printing followed the next year. In 1678 Spener put out a Latin translation of his own and appended a section on the conversion of the Jews. Three more German editions appeared by 1712. After this the *Pia Desideria* was not reprinted until the religious awakenings of the nineteenth century revived interest in the work,[19] and then it was usually put out in abridged form and in modernized German.[20]

The structure of the work is uncomplicated. It falls naturally into three parts.[21] The first part reviews the shortcomings of the church in Spener's day. Attention is called to the moral laxity in all classes of society. Sins are not taken seriously, and religious duties are performed for the most part in a merely external and superficial way. Clergy and laity are equally at fault. The second

[19] *Ibid.,* III, 253, 254.

[20] The best modernized abridgement is in *Hauptschriften Philipp Jakob Speners,* ed. Paul Grünberg, Vol. XXI of the *Bibliothek theologischer Klassiker* (Gotha: F. A. Perthes, 1889).

[21] A critical text is available in *Philipp Jakob Speners Pia Desideria,* ed. Kurt Aland (Berlin: Walter de Gruyter, 1940 and 1952), in the series "Kleine Texte für Vorlesungen und Übungen." This text has been used with Professor Aland's permission as a basis for the present edition and translation. The subheadings in square brackets have been added by the translator for the convenience of the reader.

part of the work asserts the possibility of reform. There is no justification for despair. The promises of God in the Bible and the example of the early church offer ample encouragement for the expectation of better conditions in the church. The third part of the work presents six concrete proposals for achieving the desired reform. Here Spener calls for a more extensive private and public use of the Scriptures, a larger participation and activity on the part of the laity, a realization that in Christianity doing is important as well as believing, an education of ministers that couples piety with learning, and an introduction of preaching that has edification and the inner life as its goal. Only at the end does Spener refer to John Arndt's sermons as a model for the kind of preaching he has in mind.

Before the publication of the *Pia Desideria* as a separate work in the fall of the year 1675, Spener had requested some sympathizers to write opinions or comments on what he had written. Two of these were printed as appendixes,[22] and together they are a little longer than the work on which they commented. The first of these was written by John Henry Horb, the husband of one of Spener's younger sisters and at the time a superintendent. For the most part Horb follows the order of Spener's topics and comments on them with approval or disapproval. In doing so, he tends to lose himself in details. He declares his agreement with Spener in general, but defends theological controversy and its introduction into the pulpit, takes exception to Spener's advocacy of church discipline, and is less optimistic about the possibility of reform. The second response was written by Joachim Stoll, who has already been referred to as the husband of Spener's oldest sister and as the court chaplain in Rappoltstein. He, too, comments with approval on most of Spener's analysis. However, he suggests that students

[22] See Kurt Aland, *Spener-Studien* (Berlin: Walter de Gruyter, 1943), pp. 34-40. Spener's table of contents for the two opinions is translated below after the text of the *Pia Desideria*.

would be ill advised to read the works of such medieval mystics as John Tauler and Thomas a Kempis because of the darkness in which their understanding of Christianity was still veiled, and he objects to the preference of Lewis Bayly over John Gerhard since "a secret poison" inheres in the former. Stoll also disagrees with Spener's views on the conversion of the Jews, and it was this that led Spener to append a further discussion of the topic to a later edition. While the comments of both Horb and Stoll were on the whole favorable, Spener allowed their unfavorable remarks to stand as they were written.

Much has been written about the originality or unoriginality of Spener's *Pia Desideria*. The abridgments of the text which were used in the nineteenth century often concealed the extent to which Spener himself appealed to earlier authorities and quoted from earlier books. The translation of the complete text which is here furnished (it is astonishing that the *Pia Desideria* has never appeared in English before, even in abridged form, despite its acknowledged historical significance) should help to make it clear that Spener did not think of himself as an innovator. The very title which was chosen—*Pia Desideria,* or "Pious Wishes"—had been used before, and earlier parallels for both the criticisms and the proposals can be found inside of Germany as well as outside.

A persistent claim, recently renewed, is that Spener wrote in direct imitation of Jean de Labadie's *La réformation de l'église par le pastorat* (Middelburg, 1667) and that he was not only acquainted with this work "but had it at hand on his desk, or at all events made use of it," when he was writing his *Pia Desideria.*[23] This claim has been cogently denied by Kurt Aland, who points to the more evident dependence of Spener on the men he himself cites. There are echoes of Labadie as well as of others, notably echoes of John Arndt and John Conrad Dannhauer, because these

[23] Kurt Dietrich Schmidt, "Labadie und Spener," in *Zeitschrift für Kirchengeschichte,* 46 (1928), pp. 566-583.

men, among others, represented the tradition in which Spener grew up.

Spener stands altogether in the stream of a tradition, but with the means at our disposal it is not possible to demonstrate with certainty when he was actually dependent on it. This much is clear. But it is just as clear that he represents a unique phenomenon. Countless books were written on the same theme before and after Spener. None of them, however, even approaches the *Pia Desideria* in the conciseness and clarity of its thoughts and the grasp of its goal. Countless reform proposals were made, but nobody was able to draft a boldly outlined and, in itself, complete program like Spener's. All the ideas and all the proposals for a reform of existing conditions had been present again and again before him . . . Yet nobody but Spener was capable of putting them together in the way in which we find them in the *Pia Desideria.* [24]

The appearance of the *Pia Desideria,* especially as a separate publication, called forth an immediate and enthusiastic response throughout Germany. Within a few years Spener himself received more than three hundred letters, most of them expressing favorable comment, and Spener's reform proposals became the object of further discussion in a large pamphlet literature. The theological faculty of Tübingen University publicly praised the proposal to hold student meetings for edifying conversation, and even so contentious an orthodoxist theologian as Abraham Calovius (1612-1686) wrote to Spener with warm approval. The success of the *Pia Desideria* must have been due in part to the timeliness of its appearance, the fact that many deeply concerned people were ready for and receptive to what Spener had to say. Hardly less important to its success, however, was the character and content of the work itself. Blame for existing conditions was judiciously extended to include everybody in every class. No group was isolated as the scapegoat, nor was a remedy for existing evils sought from one

[24] Aland, *Spener-Studien,* pp. 57, 58. For the whole argument see pp. 41-62.

segment of society alone. At the same time neither evils nor proposed remedies were exhaustively catalogued and described in detail, but examples were wisely chosen and set forth with restraint. Spener offered no simple panacea but called for advance toward inner spiritual renewal along a broad front.

In the process Spener presented a program which embraced virtually everything that had hitherto concerned him and that was to occupy his attention during the remainder of his life: reform of theological education, criticism of scholastic theology and theological polemics, advocacy of interconfessional toleration and understanding, emphasis on a religion of the heart as well as the head, demand for a faith that expresses itself in life and activity, cultivation of personal holiness with a tendency toward perfectionism, upgrading of the laity, recommendation of private meetings for the fostering of piety, development of the spiritual priesthood of believers, endorsement of mysticism, etc. It is hardly surprising that the initial enthusiasm for the *Pia Desideria* cooled somewhat when the implications of one or another of these planks in Spener's platform became clearer. Clergymen felt threatened in their status by the rise of the laity, professors of theology resented the brash incursion of outsiders into their academic preserve, and the complacent were disturbed by appeals for change and for departure from what was familiar, customary, and comfortable.

Spener himself soon ascribed more and more importance to the *collegia pietatis,* which were given only passing attention in his *Pia Desideria.* If the church was to be renewed, he felt, a beginning would have to be made with the remnant of true Christians in every congregation. These had to be gathered and edified in private meetings in order that they might become a leaven to leaven the whole lump. As a matter of fact, such meetings were soon being held in many places. Contrary to Spener's intention, they sometimes became divisive. There was a tendency for the meetings to develop into little churches within the church (*ecclesiolae in ecclesia*). Some members of the groups began to decry the church as "Babel," to denounce ministers as "unconverted," to refuse any longer to attend services of the church with the "godless," and to refrain from receiving the Lord's Supper at the hands of "unworthy" ministers. Donatism combined with separatism. In time malicious rumors were circulated by outsiders about what was happening in the private meetings: that women preached, that children were taught Greek and Hebrew, that wives starved their husbands at home in order to serve delicacies to the new friends they made in the meetings, that men and women stripped themselves in each other's presence to see whether they still harbored evil lusts, etc.

Such rumors were encouraged by the formation of conventicles independent of churches and ministers. In 1682 Spener tried to counteract these by changing the meeting place from private homes to churches, but he was unable to prevent the proliferation of conventicles. He was often too loyal to his sympathizers, too fearful of quenching the Spirit, too indecisive in his judgments of men to curb questionable developments. In this situation he resorted to his pen. In 1677 he wrote a tract on *Das geistliche Priesterthum* in the form of a series of questions and answers in order to expound his views on the laity and at the same time to distinguish their rights and duties from those of the clergy.[25] In 1684 he tried to counteract the growing separation from the church with his *Der Klagen über das verdorbene Christenthum Missbrauch und rechter Gebrauch.*[26] It is wrong to conclude from a recognition of the church's faults, Spener argued, that the teachings of the church are false, that it is not the true church, and that separation from its services and sacraments is justified.

---

[25] For an English translation of "The Spiritual Priesthood" see Henry E. Jacobs, *A Summary of the Christian Faith* (Philadelphia: General Council Board of Publication, 1905), pp. 581-595.

[26] For the text of "Use and Abuse of Complaints about Christianity" see *Hauptschriften Philipp Jakob Speners,* ed. Paul Grünberg, pp. 115-183.

4

After twenty years in Frankfurt, which he thought of as his second home, Spener accepted a call to Dresden, in Saxony.[27] He had grown weary of the controversies in which he had become embroiled and impatient with the lack of cooperation from the civil authorities in Frankfurt. Consequently he did not discourage the approach which was made to him to take the post of first court chaplain to Elector John George III of Saxony, and in the summer of 1686 he moved to Dresden. Spener was disappointed to discover that the elector seldom attended church—he heard Spener preach only eight times in five years—and found it necessary to rebuke the elector for his drunkenness. The consequence was that personal friction between the two men quickly developed and contributed to Spener's short stay in Dresden. His chief duty was preaching. This left him sufficient leisure to continue and even enlarge his extensive correspondence and to write for publication. It was during this period that he wrote about the hindrances to the study of theology,[28] taking up a topic touched upon in his *Pia Desideria*. Three impediments to proper study are mentioned: the false notion that theology can be apprehended by scientific study alone, the crowding out of genuine theology by the dominance of philosophy and rhetoric, and the godless life of those engaged in the study.

During his stay in Dresden, Spener made the acquaintance of a young instructor, August Herman Francke (1663-1727), who was to become, in many respects, Spener's successor as the leader of German Pietism. Together with two other instructors Francke formed what was called a *collegium philobiblicum*, a society of young teachers in the University of Leipzig for the exegetical study

[27] Cf. "Philipp Jakob Spener: sein Lebensweg von Frankfurt nach Berlin, 1666-1705," in Kurt Aland, *Kirchengeschichtliche Entwürfe* (Gütersloh: Gerd Mohn, 1960), pp. 523-542.

[28] *De impedimentis studii theologici* (1690). There is a German translation in *Hauptschriften*, pp. 184-231.

of the Bible. Partly under the influence of Spener and partly as a result of Francke's sharp experience of conversion, the society turned more and more from academic exercises to the cultivation of the inner religious life. Opposition developed in the faculty, Francke was forced out of the university, and Spener helped him get an appointment in the new Saxon university in Halle, where Francke spent the remainder of his fruitful life. It was from Halle that Francke's son later sent Henry Melchior Muhlenberg (1711-1787) to America to become the organizer of the colonial Lutheran church.[29]

Spener was also drawn during these years into a controversy between adherents and opponents of his in Hamburg. Conventicles were formed there in which, it was charged, extravagant practices were tolerated. What especially started the strife, however, was an attack by some of Spener's sympathizers on the opera as a worldly spectacle. The rigid orthodoxist John Frederick Mayer (1650-1712) defended not only opera but all theater attendance, dancing, card-playing, drinking bouts, and the like as *adiaphora,* the right use of which is permissible and only the abuse of which is forbidden. He argued in defense of theatrical performances on the ground that the Holy Spirit had appeared in the form of a dove and angels had taken on the appearance of young men. Ridicule only inflamed those who were called pietists by their opponents. They called upon Spener for help. In theory he agreed with Mayer, but in practice he leaned toward the position of his adherents, who included his brother-in-law John Henry Horb.

It was with some sense of relief that in the summer of the year 1691 Spener left Dresden for Berlin. He had been called as a member of the Lutheran consistory, as inspector or visitor of churches, and as stated preacher in the Church of St. Nicholas. Until his

[29] *The Journals of Henry Melchior Muhlenberg,* ed. and trans. T. G. Tappert and J. W. Doberstein (3 vols., Philadelphia: Muhlenberg Press, 1942-1958), I, 4-9.

death fourteen years later he remained in Berlin and was increasingly involved in the controversies which attended the spread of the pietistic movement. The existence of over five hundred controversial pamphlets dating from the last decade of the seventeenth century testifies to the extent of the strife.[30] The charge of the theological faculty of the University of Wittenberg that pietists were guilty of at least 284 heresies[31] suggests something of its bitterness. Radical excesses in the movement were ascribed to the conservative Spener, who was called a Quaker, a Rosicrucian, a chiliast, a fanatic. There was no want of extremists, and Spener invited trouble because he was reluctant to disown them.

In his last years, at the urging of friends, Spener gathered and edited about a thousand of his letters, papers, and opinions and had them published in four stout volumes, to which four other volumes were added posthumously.[32] Although the documents in the first volumes were sharply edited by Spener to remove personal allusions and questionable judgments, they represent a very important source of our knowledge of Spener himself and of early German Pietism as a whole. For contemporaries they provided casuistical guidance for all manner of questions: What makes a man a Christian? Can a Christian become perfect? Should one omit doing good if evil arises from it? What ought one to do when assailed by doubt? What is to be said about visions, ecstasies, dreams, special revelations? Is a Christian obliged to impoverish himself to help his neighbor? May a Christian wear gold and pearl ornaments with a good conscience? May he attend the theater or dance? Is sexual intercourse permitted before marriage, or

[30] Grünberg, *Philipp Jakob Spener,* I, 269.

[31] Hans-Martin Rotermund, *Orthodoxie und Pietismus* (Berlin: Evangelische Verlagsanstalt, 1960), p. 8. This study reviews these and later controversies through the eyes of Valentine Ernest Löscher.

[32] Spener, *Theologische Bedencken* (4 vols., Halle, 1700-1702); *Letzte Theologische Bedencken,* ed. Baron von Canstein (3 vols., Halle, 1711); *Consilia et Iudicia Theologica Latina,* ed. Spener's heirs (Frankfurt, 1709). These appeared in several editions, sometimes abridged.

during pregnancy in marriage? May a Protestant marry a Roman Catholic? Are the deathbed wishes of a parent binding on the children? Can an unconverted preacher proclaim God's Word as effectively as a godly preacher? What should a preacher do if he gets stuck in his sermon? May a Christian innkeeper serve his guests food and drink on Sunday? May laymen administer the Lord's Supper? Is it possible to subscribe Creeds and Confessions and still adhere to the authority of the Scriptures? These questions reflect the kinds of problems Spener was asked to solve, and at the same time they suggest the scruples which were common to pietists.

During his last years Spener served as a sponsor at the baptism of Nicholas Zinzendorf (1700-1760), thus forming a physical link with the man who became the founder (or renovator) of the Moravian church.[33] Another link was later forged between Zinzendorf and John Wesley (1703-1791), the founder of the Methodist church, who further developed Spener's view of Christian perfection.[34]

A few days before his death on February 5, 1705, Spener ordered that his coffin should not be painted black. "During my life," he was reported to have said, "I have sufficiently lamented the condition of the church; now that I am about to enter the church triumphant, I wish to be buried in a white coffin as a sign that I am dying in the hope of a better church on earth." Whether or not this report is true, it fits the spirit of the man—soft and sensitive and optimistic to the end.

In evaluating Spener and his work it has been customary to emphasize that he was primarily a reformer of Christian life, not a

[33] Cf. John R. Weinlick, *Count Zinzendorf* (Nashville: Abingdon Press, 1956).

[34] Cf. Martin Schmidt, *John Wesley, a Theological Biography, Vol. I, 1703-1738* (Nashville: Abingdon Press, 1963); Arthur W. Nagler, *Pietism and Methodism* (Nashville: Smith & Lamar, 1918); R. N. Flew, *The Idea of Perfection in Christian Theology: an Historical Study* (London: Oxford University Press, 1934).

reformer of Christian thought, that his proper place is in the history of Christian piety rather than in the history of Christian doctrine. He was by no means theologically incompetent or inarticulate, however, even if his interest in theology was practical.[35] He had an influence in the development of Christian thought without quite intending it or being fully aware of it. When challenged, Spener protested his orthodoxy—that is, his adherence to the Lutheran scholastic theology of his day. He usually employed the current theological formulations and avoided novelty of expression. At the same time, however, he was critical of the unnecessary subtleties of orthodoxist theology, of its dependence on "heathen philosophy" (Aristotle), and of all the "wood, hay, and stubble" that had been accumulated. What he regarded as "apostolic simplicity" in contrast to the learned sophistry of the seventeenth century attracted him because it could be put to effective practical use. He also inveighed on occasion against the dogmatic tyranny which was imposed by academic and ecclesiastical authority and shackled the movement of the Spirit.

Such critical observations are more prominent in Spener's private correspondence than in his published works. A shift in emphasis is nevertheless observable everywhere, both in what he wrote and in what he left unsaid. He did not deny the scholastic doctrine of the inspiration of the Scriptures, but he was more interested in their content than in their form and in their effect than in their origin. He paid more attention than most of his contemporaries to the historical context of passages of the Bible, and he was less bound by tradition in interpreting them. Spener made much of the Confessions of his church but distinguished between what was essential and what was non-essential in them. He pointed to what he regarded as errors in the Confessions—for example, that

[35] On Spener's theology see Grünberg, *Philipp Jakob Spener*, I, 383-526; Emanuel Hirsch, *Geschichte der neueren Evangelischen Theologie* (5 vols., Gütersloh: C. Bertelsmann, 1949-1954), II, 91-155.

in the Apology of the Augsburg Confession penance is called a sacrament and prayer for the dead is not forbidden. Since he looked upon the Confessions as testimonies to faith rather than as laws of faith, such shortcomings did not prevent his subscription. In his treatment of particular doctrines Spener for the most part allowed the objective statements of the scholastic theologians to stand and he put these into a more subjective orientation. His tendency was to esteem as really important only those doctrines which played a direct part in personal religious experience. This had the effect of relegating other doctrines to the realm of unnecessary ballast, and in the long run the position was theologically more revolutionary than either Spener or his opponents seemed to realize.

The difference between Lutherans and the Reformed, which occupied much of the attention of the scholastic theologians, was generally played down by Spener as a result of his emphasis on subjective faith (*fides qua creditur*) as over against objective faith (*fides quae creditur*). The Calvinistic doctrine of predestination, especially as it was framed at the Synod of Dort (1618), was attacked by him as a "horrible teaching." Characteristically it was assailed less on exegetical and doctrinal grounds than on the practical ground that it undermined Christian certainty and belief in God's love. The Reformed understanding of the Lord's Supper troubled Spener less because Lutherans and Reformed both agreed that Christ is present in the sacrament even if they did not agree on the mode of the presence. Since the Reformed with whom Spener came into contact did not share the extreme view of the Synod of Dort on predestination, he saw no reason for the current hostility between the two Protestant communions. On the contrary, he pleaded for their cooperation against their common opponent, Rome.

It is not surprising, therefore, to learn that Spener was charged by his orthodoxist critics with doctrinal laxity toward the Reformed. This charge was so expanded by later critics as to suggest that all of Spener's reform proposals were colored by the Reformed influences in his early Alsatian and Swiss environments, deepened by his reading of foreign devotional literature. Much was made of the fact that Pietism flourished in Reformed countries, like the Netherlands, before it gained a footing in the Lutheran church. The conclusion was drawn from this (and also from the emphasis on denial of self and the world) that Pietism was an "alien element" introduced into the Lutheran church from the outside, where it had its real home in the Reformed tradition and its remoter roots in the asceticism of the Middle Ages.[36] This interpretation does scant justice to the existence of the large literature, urging a reform of religious and moral life, within Lutheranism long before Spener.

According to a more recent interpretation,[37] the distinguishing feature of Spener's whole program of church reform, for which the *Pia Desideria* was the classic expression, was his rejection of the scholastic tradition and the substitution for it of the tradition of mystical spiritualism, which can be traced back through John Arndt to John Tauler and others in the late Middle Ages. Characteristic of this tradition is the central place given to regeneration (a biological image) instead of justification (a forensic image). The language of "rebirth," "new man," "inner man," "illumination," "edification," and "union of Christ with the soul" is common to Spener and to the older mystics. It expressed the mystery of the origin and growth of the Christian life, and it enjoyed a revival in the nineteenth century, beginning with F. D. Schleiermacher (1768-1834). Spener's was "an impressive attempt to define Christianity and the church anthropologically, from man's point of view, without sacrificing the absolute power of God. It

[36] Cf. Albrecht Ritschl, *Geschichte des Pietismus* (3 vols., Bonn: Marcus, 1880-1886).

[37] Martin Schmidt, "Spener und Luther," in *Luther-Jahrbuch,* Vol. XXIV (Berlin, 1957), pp. 102-129.

was an attempt to view Christian existence single-mindedly from its goal, its *eschaton,* its perfection."[88]

Like other great figures in history, Spener was a complex personality. As he was himself shaped by many forces, the influence he had on his contemporaries and on later generations was many-sided and cannot easily be comprehended in a single formula. However, the main directions of the program of reform which he set down in his *Pia Desideria* are clear. The echo of their challenge can still be detected when we read this little book today.[89]

* * *

Footnotes in the translation of the *Pia Desideria* which follows are not Spener's. Kurt Aland's critical text (see above, footnote 21) has been followed in the identification of books and tracts to which Spener referred. Except in the case of patristic references, where various texts may easily be located, English translations have been cited when such are available. Editorial interpolations in the body of the text itself are enclosed in brackets. In addition, only a few footnotes were added to clarify the meaning of things which might otherwise remain obscure to the reader. This has, of course, also been one of the purposes of this introduction.

There is a measure of monotony in Spener's style of writing, and this could not be entirely overcome in the translation without departing from what he wrote. On the other hand, an effort has been made to remove the obscurities and simplify the cumbersome constructions which are even more characteristic of Spener's German than of the German of most of his contemporaries.

T. G. T.

[88] *Ibid.,* pp. 128, 129.

[89] Evidence of continuing interest may be seen in the unpublished doctoral dissertation by Dale Weaver Brown, "The Problem of Subjectivism in Pietism: A Redefinition with Special Reference to the Theology of Philipp Jakob Spener and August Hermann Francke" (Evanston, Garrett Theological Seminary and Northwestern University, 1962).

PIA DESIDERIA

or

Heartfelt Desire

for a God-pleasing Reform

of the true Evangelical Church,

Together with Several Simple Christian Proposals

Looking Toward this End

*

With Appended Comments on the Same,

Very Useful for Edification,

by Two Christian Theologians

*

By Philip Jacob Spener, Th.D.

Minister and Senior of the Clergy
in Frankfurt am Main

[SALUTATION AND
CIRCUMSTANCES OF WRITING]

To the faithful leaders and pastors of the whole Evangelical Christian church:

May the Father of light and Giver of all good things grant you, my Fathers and Brethren, beloved and esteemed in Christ Jesus, our chief shepherd,

Enlightened eyes of understanding to discern what is the hope of our calling, what are the riches of God's glorious inheritance for his saints, and how boundless is God's strength in us who believe that his mighty power is effectual;

Diligence and zeal to be of good cheer and to strengthen others who may grow faint;

Strength and courage (with the weapons of our calling, which are not fleshly but mighty for God) to destroy the strongholds and frustrate the assaults on, and all the defenses which are raised against, the knowledge of God, to take all reason captive in obedience to Christ, and to be ready to punish all disobedience when the obedience of the believers is fulfilled;

Blessing and success to observe with joy that the Word that goes forth from God's mouth, as the rain and the snow come down from heaven, shall not return to God empty but shall accomplish that which he purposes and prosper in the thing for which he sent it,[1] and to behold how the earth, cultivated through your ministry, produces first the blade, then the ear, then the full grain in the ear;[2]

Complete pleasure in the knowledge that through your ministry the name of God is hallowed, his kingdom extended, and his will is done,[3] and that the salvation of many souls, the peace of your own consciences, and ultimately your eternal glory are achieved to the honor of his holy name.

Fathers and Brethren, beloved in the dear Lord:

When, a half-year ago,[4] the publisher[5] of the new edition of Arndt's postil[6] asked me to write a preface for that precious work, I ventured, in the brief time available, to set down in this preface most of the things that had again and again sorely distressed me, troubled my conscience, and given me concern as long as by God's will and grace I have labored in his vineyard. I was aware meanwhile that countless others joined me in my laments and often poured out their sorrowful complaints in one another's ears.

The wretched conditions which we deplore are known to all. Nobody is forbidden to shed tears over them, be it in private or in places where others may behold the tears and may thereby be moved to sympathy and cooperation. Where one sees distress and sickness it is natural to look about for remedies. The precious spiritual body of Christ is now afflicted with distress and sickness. Since in certain respects it is committed to the care of every individual and at the same time to all and sundry together, and since we must all be members of the body and hence should not regard

[1] Cf. Isa. 55:10-11.

[2] Cf. Mark 4:28.

[3] Cf. Matt. 6:9-10.

[4] In the spring of the year 1675.

[5] Johann David Zunner, formerly in Copenhagen in the service of an Amsterdam book dealer, established a business of his own in Frankfurt, where he became one of the leading publishers.

[6] Sermons by Johann Arndt (1555-1621) on the Gospels of the church year, first published in 1616 under the title *Postilla, Auslegung der Sonntagsevangelien.*

affliction anywhere in the body as alien to us, it is therefore incumbent on us to see to it that medicine which is suited to its cure
be found and applied.

In former times the most effective remedy was the convening
in councils of the principal leaders of churches and delegates from
all particular churches of consequence in order to deliberate about
the common infirmity. Would to God that we were now in a position to entertain the hope of accomplishing something in this way!
How often and anxiously have devout men desired this! If we wait
for this to happen, however, we shall die before our wish is realized, and reform will always be postponed (I do not know how
responsibly) to the uncertain future.

I am not sure whether, for want of a council, it would not be a
suitable remedy at this time if Christian ministers would themselves not only write to one another in the fear of the Lord but
also discuss these important matters openly with one another in
print and carefully ponder whatever may be useful to the people
of God. In this way, for the sake of report and reflection, the
thoughts of colleagues may be made known to others who are concerned about the work of the Lord.

Inasmuch as other earnest Christian theologians have long since
begun to do this very thing here and there in their published writings, I am not the first to give open expression to such a desire
and to make suggestions concerning it. Yet I might properly have
hesitated to sally forth with my simple thoughts, since in the kingdom of the Lord as well as in the kingdom of the world suffrage
must be granted according to the station and dignity of persons,
and on this basis I must in all fairness regard myself as among
the least. However, this order need not be observed in the Christian church any more than in the world, where for special reasons
the practice has been introduced in some meetings to begin the
voting at the bottom and also to give the lower ranks opportunity
to speak their minds without prejudice and with more freedom

than is granted the upper ranks, who with their more mature reflection are allowed the honor of amending the proposals which the others make. I have therefore concluded that I cannot well be charged with presumption for writing what I have in this preface (as God is my witness) in tender love toward the people of God and a desire not to omit anything that may serve the divine honor.

Lest I rely on my own judgment alone and allow the very things that would do the church more harm than good to see the light of day, I laid my essay before my dearly beloved colleagues and fellow ministers here,[7] for in view of the approaching fair it was not possible to communicate with people outside the city.[8] Since the spirits of the prophets are subject to the prophets,[9] I not only read my essay to them word for word but also gave them full liberty (which is theirs anyhow) to take fraternal exception to what I had written whenever they deemed this necessary. I gladly inserted several things, useful for edification, that they contributed. As for the rest, they greatly encouraged me by approving everything included in the essay and by heartily expressing the wish that God might not fail to bless his work. Thereupon I gave the preface to the printer in the name of the Lord.

Since it was not possible for them to buy Arndt's postil, either because it was too expensive or because they already had an earlier edition of the postil, many good people expressed a desire to see this preface available separately and asked that it be so printed. The publisher even received letters from other cities in which some good people declared that if he would not publish the preface as a separate book they would have it printed themselves. Accordingly when the publisher conferred with me about this, I was not unwilling to proceed at once with the preparation of a new edi-

[7] Since 1566 Spener had been senior of the ministerium (i.e., presiding officer among all the ministers) in Frankfurt am Main.
[8] There was no time before the annual spring fair, or market, for which the book was being rushed through the press.
[9] Cf. I Cor. 12:10; I John 4:1.

tion, especially because there is always danger that typographical errors will creep in if the preface is reprinted elsewhere.

I was the more ready to do this because several months after the original printing I received a very useful and edifying comment which had been written on request by a Christian superintendent[10] who is laboring faithfully in the vineyard of the Lord. No sooner had he sent his comment to me than I began to hope that its publication would prove more useful than my own insignificant work. The author doubted whether he ought to attach his name to his writing not only because he was disinclined to seek his own honor but also because a publication may do more good and be judged solely on its own merits if attention is not directed to the author's involvement and intention. However, he is not afraid to be identified if it is deemed advantageous and necessary to the church that this be done, for he takes pains to allow God's honor and its promotion to be his sole purpose and the rule in all that he does.

Just as I was finishing with this essay and the fair was about to open, another comment came into my hands. It was by another Christian theologian,[11] a well-versed man, wonderfully endowed by God, equipped by long experience in matters advantageous to the common welfare, and one whom I have always respected as a father. As soon as I read it I was filled with a desire that this, too, be shared in print with other people. I was hindered, however, by the fact that I did not have the express permission of this dear man, and there was no time, with the fair at hand, to request his permission and wait for it inasmuch as he lives at a distance. Accordingly I discussed the matter with sev-

[10] Johann Heinrich Horb, Spener's brother-in-law and since 1679 superintendent in Windsheim, wrote *Erfordertes Bedencken Auff Hn. Philipp Jacob Speners ... Teutsche Vorrede zu dess seligen Arndii Postill.*

[11] Joachim Stoll, 1615-1678, Spener's teacher and brother-in-law who had been court chaplain in Rappoltstein after 1647, wrote *Ferneres Bedencken Eines andern Christlichen und Wohlerfahrenen Theologi.*

eral intimate friends. Since this dear father's consuming zeal for the furtherance of the church's common welfare was sufficiently known to me, and no important reason occurred to any of us which might have made him unwilling to have his comment published, it was finally decided that in the name of the Lord I should put what he had written in an appendix. There was no consensus among us about using his name, and therefore I have not ventured to do so in order that if, contrary to expectation, he should object to the publication, the blame might be minimized by the omission of his name. Confident that he will not deny my request, I ask him here not to take amiss my boldness in making public what he sent, although I did not have his permission to do so, but in friendly fashion to ascribe my action to the desire to be of service to everybody, which is indeed the source of my boldness.

In accordance with the liberty that must in fairness be allowed us, I have left the comments as they stand here, even if they depart from my way of thinking in one or two places. Thus the reader will be free to ponder the matter thoroughly and in every case choose what seems to him to be best founded. Herewith, therefore, these pages, now supplemented by other pious works, are once again (that is, for the second time) being brought to light through the press. They have no other purpose than to be edifying—if not to many, then at least to a few. If nothing else is accomplished, it is hoped that through these pages other enlightened men, who are more highly endowed by God, may be encouraged earnestly to undertake this most important work of advancing true godliness, for a time make this their principal task, and thoroughly consider the devising, the testing, and the practical implementation of salutary remedies which conform with the rule of the Word of God.

Some time ago the late Dr. Dorsche proposed[12] that in order

---

[12] Johann Dorsche, 1579-1659, Spener's teacher in Strasbourg, made his proposal in *Admirandorum Jesu Christi Septenarius* (Hamburg, 1646).

to maintain orthodoxy it would be of advantage to introduce and carry on a fraternal and confidential correspondence among the professors. Not a little could be hoped for from this. As this proposal appeared to be good, useful, and profitable for the maintenance of pure teaching, so it ought not to be less useful, with reference to the practice and the government of the church, to carry on just such a correspondence among ministers appointed to ecclesiastical offices as well as academic men and to attempt to advance the cause partly through private and partly through public writings.

Let us, all of us together, now do diligently what we have been appointed to do, namely, to feed the flock which God has bought with his own blood and therefore at a very great price.

Let us remember, dear Fathers and Brethren, what we promised to God when we were set apart for our ministries and what must consequently be our concern.

Let us remember the rigorous reckoning which faces us at the hands of him who will call us to account for the souls which have in any way been neglected.

Let us remember that in the last judgment we shall not be asked how learned we were and whether we displayed our learning before the world; to what extent we enjoyed the favor of men and knew how to keep it; with what honors we were exalted and how great a reputation in the world we left behind us; or how many treasures of earthly goods we amassed for our children and thereby drew a curse upon ourselves. Instead, we shall be asked how faithfully and with how childlike a heart we sought to further the kingdom of God; with how pure and godly a teaching and how worthy an example we tried to edify our hearers amid the scorn of the world, denial of self, taking up of the cross, and imitation of our Savior; with what zeal we opposed not only error but also wickedness of life; or with what constancy and cheerfulness we endured the persecution or adversity thrust upon us by the manifestly godless world or by false brethren, and amid such suffering praised our God.

Let us therefore be diligent in investigating ever more deeply our own shortcomings and those of the rest of the church in order that we may learn to know our sicknesses, and then with a fervent invocation of God for the light of his Spirit let us also search for and ponder over the remedies.

Let us not leave it at that, however, but let everybody seek, as he is able in his own congregation, to introduce what we have found to be beneficial and necessary. For what is the value of consultation except to serve as a testimony against us whenever we do not desire to live up to what we have found to be good?

If we have to suffer somewhat at the hands of people who disagree with us, let us take it as a reassuring sign that our work is pleasing to the Lord, inasmuch as he allows it to be put to such a test, and meanwhile let us not grow weary on this account and let up in our zeal.

Let us begin by putting ourselves at the disposal especially of those who are still willing to accept what is done for their edification. If everybody in his own congregation makes provision for these above all others, they may little by little grow to such a measure of godliness that they will be shining examples to others. In time, then, by God's grace we may also gradually attract those who at present seem to be lost in order that they, too, may finally be won. All of my suggestions are aimed quite exclusively at first helping those who are tractable, at doing all that is needful for their edification. Once this is accomplished and made the foundation, sternness toward the disobedient may bear more fruit.

Let us not abandon all hope before we have set our hands to the task. Let us not lay down our rod and staff if we do not have the desired success at once. What is impossible for men remains possible for God. Eventually God's hour must come, if only we wait for it. Our fruit, like other fruit, must be borne in patience, and the fruit in others must be cultivated by us with perseverance. The work of the Lord is accomplished in wondrous ways, even as he is himself wonderful. For this very reason his work is done in complete secrecy, yet all the more surely, provided we do not relax our efforts. If God does not give you the pleasure of seeing the result of your work quickly, perhaps he intends to hide it from you, lest you become too proud of it. Seeds are there, and you may think they are unproductive, but do your part in watering them, and ears will surely sprout and in time become ripe.

In addition to continuing our work, then, let us commend the matter to our heavenly Father, pray fervently to him, and be content with such success in our work as he may be pleased to have us see. With sincere devotion let us therefore help one another to wrestle with prayer and supplication, that here and there God may open up one door after another to his Word, that we may proclaim the mystery of Christ fruitfully, that we may do so cheerfully and speak in a befitting manner, and that we may glorify his name with our teaching, our life, and our suffering.

Assuring you of this my poor but fervent prayer, my request, my hope, and at the same time my fraternal intercession, I commit all of you to the faithful favor and guidance of the Lord God.

Frankfurt am Main
September 8, 1675

PHILIP JACOB SPENER, TH.D.

[PART I]

[CONSPECTUS OF CORRUPT CONDITIONS IN THE CHURCH]

To all who seek the Lord: grace, light, and salvation from God our heavenly Father, through Jesus Christ, in the Holy Spirit.

If, in accordance with our Savior's admonition[1] to interpret the signs of the times and their character, we observe the present condition of Christendom as a whole through Christian and somewhat enlightened eyes, we may well burst forth with the plaintive words of Jeremiah 9:1, "O that my head were waters, and my eyes a fountain of tears, that I might weep day and night for the slain of the daughter of my people." Even in an early golden age of the church a dear old father could say, "Good God, for what times hast thou preserved me!"[2] In our day we have much more reason to repeat such words, or rather to sigh them, for the greater the distress the more one is at a loss for words.

I shall not now speak of the distress of those members of the Christian church who are hidden and must seek their salvation with fear and trembling in the face of great danger: those who dwell among heretics in the Babylonian captivity of anti-Christian Rome; those who live in Greece and the Orient under the equally severe tyranny of the Turks, some in unbelievable ignorance and

[1] Matt. 16:3.
[2] Polycarp, quoted in Eusebius, *Ecclesiastical History*, V, 20.

others mingling errors and shocking scandals with the truth; and those who are in churches in which there are many false doctrines because, although they have rejected the pope, they have not attained purity in their teaching. The wretchedness of such people cannot be recalled by a godly soul without profound emotion.

If we limit ourselves to our Evangelical church, which according to its outward confession embraces the precious and pure gospel, brought clearly to light once again during the previous century through that blessed instrument of God, Dr. Luther, and in which alone we must therefore recognize that the true church is visible, we cannot turn our eyes upon it without having quickly to cast them down again in shame and distress.

When we look at its outward condition we must confess that for a long time the kingdoms and lands which are attached to this church have again and again, although to different degrees and in different times, experienced those calamities of pestilence, famine, and continuous or often recurring wars in which, according to the Scriptures,[3] the righteous God is wont to indicate and bear witness to his wrath. Yet I do not regard such afflictions as the worst. In fact, I count them a blessing, for through them God has preserved many of his own and has to some extent averted the harm that would have resulted if people had been driven to deeper despair by uninterrupted external prosperity.

Although not easily discerned by human eyes, the spiritual misery of our poor church is incomparably more grievous and dangerous. And this principally for two reasons.

The first is the persecutions which true doctrine must suffer at the hands, especially, of the anti-Christian Babel.[4] To be sure, persecutions are nothing less than a glorious means whereby the growth of the church has often been furthered. We find that since apostolic days the Christian church has never been in a better and

---

[3] E.g., Matt. 24:6-8.
[4] Rome, or the Roman Catholic church.

more glorious condition before God than when it was subjected to the most terrible persecutions. Then its gold lay constantly in the smelting furnace, whose flames did not permit the accretion of dross or else quickly consumed it.[5] But we observe two things in the persecutions of former times, and these grieve us the more.

For one thing, when the devil realized that his violent and bloody persecutions accomplished nothing, for many people were so glad to suffer a quick, even if terrible, martyrdom that they rushed headlong to their death rather than shrink from it, he grew shrewder and started a different kind of persecution. He assailed adherents of the true religion with lingering, long lasting tribulations, sometimes by means of threats and at other times by means of promises and visions of worldly glory, more often by the removal or expulsion of faithful ministers, in order to entice people away from the known truth and at the very least to get their children and descendants to return to false religion. This kind of persecution, which was employed in ancient times by the heathen Emperor Julian the Apostate, was much more dangerous to the church, as Rufinus clearly shows,[6] than the earlier, fiercer ones, in spite of the fact that less blood was shed. In former times the Roman pope also preferred to employ this method against us, and to put it into execution he often incited heads of government who were attached to the devotion of his see. More harm was done in this way than if fire and sword had been taken in hand.

Another thing follows from this. Persecutions have at all times had the effect that Christians have multiplied and consequently that the blood of martyrs has been a powerful fertilizer in the church, so that while believers seemed in the eyes of the world to be overcome, they actually triumphed and gained one victory after another (which, among others, my highly esteemed friend in the Lord, Dr. Christian Korthold, has clearly set forth in the light of

[5] Cf. Ezek. 22:18-22; I Cor. 3:13-15.
[6] Rufinus, *Ecclesiastical History*, X, 33.

church history in his edifying *Creutz- und Gedult-spiegel,*[7] recently published here). Nevertheless, by means of persecution the Roman papacy has hitherto actually recovered kingdoms and provinces in which the truth of the gospel had been extensively accepted or in which many seeds of it had been disseminated. The consequence has been that there are no longer any confessors, or only a few confessors, of Evangelical truth in these lands. Moreover, as the few who remain gradually die off, the papacy can look forward to the achievement of its goal. Thus, while the external conception of the true church is being reduced to ever narrower compass, the boundaries of the papacy are being extended.

Accordingly we have greater reason to lament and grieve over such unhappy results of the persecutions than over the sufferings in the persecutions themselves. Joshua once felt like this when his previously victorious army suffered a reverse, though a minor one, at the hands of the men of Ai.[8] So also did the Israelites when they were twice forced to flee before the Benjaminites and so many of them were slain that it seemed the Lord would depart from them on account of the sins they had committed, whereupon they sought him again in humble penitence.[9] Such power which God allows to opponents is a sure sign that our church as a whole is not in the condition in which it should be, that there is very much gold that glitters from the outside but does not meet the test when it is smelted.

The second and principal reason for the lament is the fact that almost everywhere there is something wanting in the church, except that in his inexhaustible goodness God has not taken away his Word and holy sacraments. Where is there an estate[10] of

[7] Christian Korthold, *Creutz- und Gedult-spiegel, aus Göttlicher Schrifft und der alten und neuen Kirchen-Historie fürgestellet* (Frankfurt, 1676). Spener sought Korthold's advice when he received his call to Dresden.

[8] Josh. 7:2-26.

[9] Judg. 20:21-28.

[10] A social and political class, as the discussion which follows makes clear.

which we can boast that it is in such condition as Christian precepts demand?

[Defects in Civil Authorities]

When we observe the political estate and behold those in it who, according to the divine prophecy (Isa. 49:23) made in the New Testament, should be foster fathers and nursing mothers,[11] how few there are who remember that God gave them their scepters and staffs in order that they use their power to advance the kingdom of God! Instead, most of them, as is customary with great lords, live in those sins and debaucheries which usually go along with court life and are regarded as virtually inseparable from it, while other magistrates[12] are intent on seeking their own advantage. From their manner of life one must conclude with sighs that few of them know what Christianity is, to say nothing of their being Christians and practicing the Christian life. How many of them there are who do not concern themselves at all with what is spiritual, who hold with Gallio[13] that they have nothing to do with anything but the temporal! Even among those who still take an interest in the first table[14] and mean to be of service to the church, how many there are who put their emphasis on maintaining the traditional pure religion and preventing the introduction of false religion, which is far from being all that is required of them! In fact, in how many instances must one fear that their apparent zeal for our religion stems from a factious spirit or a design to further some political interest rather than from a love of truth! How ungrateful many of them are to the great goodness of God, who liberated them from the stern yoke of papal clericalism and showed them what it was like—a clericalism which those (includ-

[11] In Rev. 3:9 there is an allusion to Isa. 49:23.
[12] *Magistraten*, i.e., civil rulers.
[13] Cf. Acts 18:12-17.
[14] The first three of the Ten Commandments which deal with duties to God.

ing crowned heads) who lived several hundred years ago sufficiently experienced. Although their power was given to them in
order to promote and not to suppress the church, they abuse this
power with an irresponsible caesaropapism, and whenever some
ministers of the church, moved by God, propose to do something
that is good, they arbitrarily obstruct it. It is to be lamented that
in some places congregations are better off where they are under a
ruler of a different religious persuasion[15] than are those who live
under a ruler of their own religion but experience more hindrance
than help from him. The former may have much to endure, yet
they may not be altogether prevented from the practice of that
which contributes to edification.

[Defects in the Clergy]

Distressing as conditions in the political estate are, we preachers
in the ecclesiastical estate cannot deny that our estate is also thoroughly corrupt. Thus most of the deterioration in the church has
its source in the two higher estates. Long ago an old church father
recommended that this conclusion be drawn: *"Quemadmodum
videns arborem foliis pallentibus, marcidam, intelligis, quod ali-
quam culpam habeat circa radicem: ita cum videris populum in-
disciplinatum, sine dubio cognosce, quod sacerdotium ejus non est
sanctum";* that is, just as you know, when you see a tree whose
leaves are faded and withering, that there is something wrong
with the roots, so, when you see that the people are undisciplined,
you must realize that no doubt their priests are not holy.[16] I gladly
acknowledge the holiness of our divine calling, and I know that
God has kept some in our ranks who take the work of the Lord

[15] On the European continent at the close of the seventeenth century Lutherans
sometimes lived under Reformed rulers, Reformed under Lutheran rulers,
Protestants under Roman Catholic rulers, etc.

[16] Chrysostom, *Homilies on the Gospel of St. Matthew,* 38. Spener quotes in
Latin and German versions.

seriously. Nor am I of a mind to go to extremes, as Praetorius[17] does, and throw out the child with the bath. However, the all-seeing Knower of our hearts beholds with what sadness of soul I often reflect on this and now write these lines: I cannot say anything else than that we preachers in our estate need reformation as much as any estate can ever need it. How common it was for God, whenever he planned a reformation, to begin it with the ecclesiastical estate—for example, under pious kings in the Old Testament. I do not exclude myself from the number of those in our estate who are lacking in the reputation we ought to have before God and the church. On the contrary, I recognize more and more how deficient I myself am, and I am prepared to be fraternally corrected by others. Indeed, nothing grieves me more than this: that I can hardly see how, in the face of such frightful corruption, such a one as I am can possibly recover a good conscience.

We must confess not only that men are to be found here and there in our estate who are guilty of open scandals but also that there are fewer than may at first appear who do not really understand and practice true Christianity (which consists of more than avoiding manifest vices and living an outwardly moral life). Although, according to the common estimate of men and as seen through eyes captivated by the fashion of the world, they may seem to be blameless, yet their lives reflect (subtly, to be sure, but none the less plainly) a worldly spirit, marked by carnal pleasure, lust of the eye, and arrogant behavior, and so it is evident that they have never taken even the first practical principle of Christianity seriously, namely, denial of self.

Behold how they seek promotions, shift from parish to parish, and engage in all sorts of machinations! Look with ever so loving eyes, illuminated by the light of the Spirit! One will surely

[17] Several men wrote under the pseudonym of Stephan Praetorius. The reference here is probably to Christian Hohburg, who wrote *Spiegel der Misbräuche beym Predig-Amt* (1644) and *Ministerii Lutherani Purgatio: Das ist Lutherischer Pfaffenputzer* (1648).

discover that many, of whom in Christian love one would like to think differently, are at bottom the same, that although they themselves do not realize it they are still stuck fast in the old birth and do not actually possess the true marks of a new birth. In many places Paul would still complain, "They all look after their own interests, not those of Jesus Christ" (Phil. 2:21).

Where it is recognized, such conduct causes great scandal. But greater scandal is caused when it is not recognized for what it is, when people (who according to the corruption of our nature always prefer to judge by examples rather than by precept) get the notion that what they see in their preachers must be real Christianity and that they ought not hold it against them. Most distressing of all, however, is the fact that the lives of many such preachers and the absence in them of the fruits of faith indicate that they are themselves wanting in faith. What they take to be faith and what is the ground of their teaching is by no means that true faith which is awakened through the Word of God, by the illumination, witness, and sealing of the Holy Spirit, but is a human fancy. To be sure, as others have acquired knowledge in their fields of study, so these preachers, with their own human efforts and without the working of the Holy Spirit, have learned something of the letter of the Scriptures, have comprehended and assented to true doctrine, and have even known how to preach it to others, but they are altogether unacquainted with the true, heavenly light and the life of faith.

It is not my intention to conclude from this that no good has been accomplished through such persons and their work, nor that true faith and a true conversion may not have been brought about in somebody through them, for the Word does not receive its divine power from the person of the one who proclaims it but has this power in itself. Accordingly Paul rejoiced in Philippians 1:15-18 that Christ was preached by some "from envy and rivalry," but we cannot suppose that those who preached thus were therefore loving, reborn children of God. Paul would not have had occasion to rejoice, however, if such persons, in addition to doing themselves harm in their sermons, benefited nobody else through them. No reasonable Christian will deny that those who do not themselves have true and godly faith cannot, as they ought, perform the duties of their office and through the Word awaken faith in their hearers. Not to mention that such persons are unfitted to pray so as to be heard (through which a godly preacher causes many to be blessed), they cannot possess the wisdom which is demanded of those who are to teach others with all necessary urgency and to guide them on the way of salvation. I have no doubt that we would soon have an altogether different church if most of us ministers were of such a sort that we could unblushingly say to our congregations with Paul, "Be imitators of me, as I am of Christ" (I Cor. 11:1).

On the contrary, we find that not a small number of preachers regard as unimportant what the apostle mentioned to the Ephesians as something long since learned, namely, that "in Jesus there is righteous conduct" (Eph. 4:21).[18] Consequently the common conception of the art of being saved, as most people imagine it, is not in accordance with the divine institution. If the preacher himself does not know this, how are his hearers to be brought to the point of recognizing what is necessary?

I am alarmed and ashamed whenever I think of the fact that the teaching of an earnest, inner godliness is so unfamiliar and strange to some people that those who zealously cultivate such godliness can hardly escape being suspected as secret papists, Weigelians,[19] or Quakers. In his time the sainted Dr. Balthasar Meissner,[20] who was respected for the purity of his doctrine, com-

---

[18] Instead of "upright conduct," Eph. 4:21 actually refers to "truth" in Jesus.

[19] Followers of Valentin Weigel, 1533-1588, a German mystic and pantheist. In the seventeenth century the label "Weigelian" was attached to anyone who was regarded as untrustworthy, heterodox, or antiecclesiastical.

[20] Balthasar Meisner, 1587-1626, was professor of theology in Wittenberg during the last thirteen years of his life.

plained that one could hardly avoid the suspicion of Weigelianism
or attachment to neo-sectarian teaching if one promoted godliness
with proper zeal and constantly admonished the practice of what is
taught. My dearly beloved brother-in-law Dr. John Lewis Hartmann recently lamented this in section 3 of his pastoral theology[21]
(which useful work I am especially eager to see printed soon in
one volume), and he reproduces the verses that heap such a slan-
derous suspicion on that worthy man, the sainted Dr. John Gerhard.[22]

> The man who vigorously promotes zeal for piety
> In this age, while also treating sacred theology,
> Is counted a Rosicrucian or a Weigelian,
> And the stigma of shameful heresy is attached to him.
>
> Foul calumny I suspected that he spread
> And credibility with his trifling gained.
> O blind intellects of men! Blind hearts!
> Frail judgment without power of discernment!
>
> First learn, I pray, who really is Weigelian,
> Discover first, I pray, who is a Rosicrucian.
> As rays of the sun scatter clouds in the sky,
> May brighter light distinguish true from false!

What greater evidence of calamity and corruption can there well
be than to seek occasion for suspicion and evil report in things
that properly deserve praise? Here the words apply, "If the foun-
dations are destroyed, what can the righteous do?"[23]

[21] Johann Ludwig Hartmann, *Pastorale Evangelicum seu instructio plenior
ministrorum verbi* (1678). Hartmann, 1640-1680, was superintendent in
Rothenburg ob der Tauber.

[22] Johann Gerhard, 1582-1637, was the leading Lutheran systematic theologian
of the seventeenth century, best known for his extensive work *Loci communes
theologici* (1609-1622). The verses which are quoted appear in Hartmann,
op. cit., II, 232, without giving the source. They are here translated from the
Latin without attempting to imitate the original rhythm.

[23] Ps. 11:3.

Numerous are those who do not recognize the ruin of Joseph[24] in many areas. They think that the church is in a most blessed condition as long as we are not hard pressed by opponents of a false religion and enjoy outward peace. They do not see the dangerous wounds at all. How, then, can they bind them up and heal them?

Controversies are not the only or the most important thing, although knowledge of them properly belongs to the study of theology. Not only should we know what is true in order to follow it, but we should also know what is false in order to oppose it. However. not a few stake almost everything on polemics. They think that everything has turned out very well if only they know how to give answer to the errors of the papists, the Reformed, the Anabaptists, etc. They pay no attention to the fruits of those articles of faith which we presumably still hold in common with them or of those rules of morality which are acknowledged by us all. The complaint of the ancient and experienced church father Gregory Nazianzen about such quarrelsomeness in his time is very penetrating (Epistle 21, or Epistle 1 in the Greek edition).[25] The sainted Dr. Christopher Scheibler not improperly applied the complaint to our time in the remarkable and excellent preface to his handbook of practical theology,[26] also reprinted as the preface to his useful work *Aurifodina.*[27] Gregory wrote: *"Omnes uno hoc nomine pii sumus, quia alii alios impietatis condemnamus,"* that is, we are all godly people for this one reason that each one of us condemns the rest as godless. Again: *"Malos & bonos non vitae sed dissidii vel concordis doctrinae signo notamus,"* that is, we judge who are good and who are evil, not according to their life but according to their doctrinal agreement or disagreement with us.

[24] Cf. Amos 6:6.

[25] *Epistles,* 1. Gregory was a bishop and theologian of the fourth century.

[26] Christoph Scheibler, *Manuale ad theologiam practicam* (Frankfurt, 1630).

[27] *Aurifodina theologica, oder Theologische und geistliche Gold-Grube* (1664). "Aurifodina" means gold mine.

Again: *"Quod nonnulli sunt qui de levibus rebus, nec quicquam utilitatis habentibus, digladiantur, sociosque mali quoscunque possunt admodum stulte temereque adsciscunt, hisque omnibus deinde fides praetexitur, atque illustre hoc nomen privatis illorum contentionibus dissidiisque convellitur"*; that is, there are some who quarrel about trivial and useless things, rashly and foolishly claim as many adherents as they can find, and then put up a defense as if the faith were at stake; thus this excellent name is weakened by their own strife and contention.

Who, judging by appearances, will not concede that the dear church father must rise up again in our day because he finds sufficient cause for such complaint? Hence it was probably necessary for Dr. David Chytraeus, who well knew what was best for the church, to deliver his oration[28] to all students several times a year—his oration *de studio Theologiae non rixis disputationum sed exercitiis pietatis potius calendo,* that is, that the study of theology should be carried on not by the strife of disputations but rather by the practice of piety. The sainted Rostock theologian Dr. John Affelmann had the same purpose in mind when (according to the witness of his faithful disciple, the sainted Henry Varenius, in his *Christliche Rettung,* p. 149[29]) he spoke thus to the students of theology at an academic affair:[30]

We do not hesitate to declare accursed those who hold in low esteem an earnest striving after sincere piety and a careful cultivation of the inner man but think that the apex of theology consists of disputing. As Bernard says in his twenty-fourth sermon on the Song of Solomon, they give their tongues to God but their souls to the devil. [31] We know that Christ is the way, the truth, and the life

[28] David Chytraeus, *Oratio de studio Theologiae* (Wittenberg, 1581).

[29] Heinrich Varenius, *Christliche, Schrifftmässige, wohlgegründete Rettung der vier Bücher vom wahren Christenthum* (2nd ed.; Lüneburg, 1689).

[30] Johann Affelmann, *Syllabus exercitationum Theologicarum de praecipuis quibusdam christianae religionis articulis* (Rostock, 1620). The quotation is reproduced by Spener first in the original Latin and then in German translation.

[31] Bernard of Clairvaux, *Sermons on the Song of Songs,* XXIV, 8.

(John 14:6), and these together, not separately. He is the way on account of his life, and we should imitate this life with earnest zeal; he is the truth on account of his teaching, and we should embrace this teaching with faithful hearts; he is the life on account of his merit, and we should take hold of this merit with true faith.

How much better it would be if more diligent consideration were given to these things!

Although by God's grace we still have pure doctrine derived from the Word of God, we cannot deny that much that is alien, useless, and reminiscent of the world's wisdom has here and there been introduced gradually into theology. There is more danger in this than one might imagine. The illuminating words which Luther addressed to the people in Erfurt ought to be borne in our minds (Tom. 2, Altenb., p. 160b):[32] "Beware! Satan has the intention of detaining you with unnecessary things and thus keeping you from those which are necessary. Once he has gained an opening in you of a hand-breadth, he will force in his whole body together with sacks full of useless questions, as he formerly did in the universities by means of philosophy." Here we hear that no little damage is done when one tries to be smart and clever without the Scriptures or beyond them. Nor is there want of examples to substantiate this.

Compare the writings of our dear Luther, in which he expounds the Word of God or treats articles of the Christian faith, with the still extant works of many other theologians who lived in and shortly after his time or with a majority of the books being published today. To speak candidly, in the former one will assuredly encounter and experience great spiritual power, together with wisdom presented with the utmost simplicity, while the latter will seem to be quite empty in contrast, and in the newer books one

[32] Reference is to Vol. II of the Altenburg edition of Martin Luther's works. See the Weimar edition of Luther's works (hereafter referred to as *WA*). 10[II], 165, 166: "Epistle or Instruction from the Saints to the Church in Erfurt," 1522.

will find more materials of showy human erudition, of artificial posturing, and of presumptuous subtleties in matters in which we should not be wise beyond the Scriptures. I wonder if our sainted Dr. Luther, were he to be raised up, would not find fault with one thing and another in our universities for which he vigorously upbraided the schools of his own time.

To be sure, this complaint is not new. Dr. David Chytraeus, that splendid man who perceived the shortcomings in the churches ahead of many others and who because of his superior experience and Christian wisdom was often called upon by king and princes to organize churches and schools,[33] made similar complaints during the last century in a letter to Jerome Menzel (in Epist. p. 348):[34]

> Would to God that we might accustom our own and our hearers' hearts and minds to the fear of the Lord, to repentance and conversion, to terror because of sin before the wrath and judgment of God, and to the practice of true godliness, righteousness, and love of God and neighbor rather than to quarrelsome disputatiousness, from which it is evident that the sophistry which was characteristic of former times has not been overcome but has simply been shifted and transferred to other questions and disputes.

Again, in a letter to another, dated *Joh. Judicem:*[35]

> It pains me that, after theology was hardly freed from the darkness of papistic sophistry, it has reverted to such an extent into a new sophistry of useless and impertinent questions. After all, the Christian religion does not consist of learning or of the sharpness of impertinent questions, which are being raised all too often in our time, but it consists of this, that from his Word we have a right knowledge of the true God and of our Savior Jesus Christ, that we inwardly fear

[33] David Chytraeus, 1531-1600, was asked by the dukes of Mecklenburg to reorganize the University of Rostock and by the Austrian estates to prepare a new church order. He also participated in the meetings at Torgau and Bergen at which the Formula of Concord (1577) was given its final form.

[34] Letter to Hieronymus Menzel, superintendent in Eisleben, in *Epistolae* (Hannover, 1614), p. 348.

[35] Letter dated "on the day of John the Evangelist, 1572," *ibid.*, pp. 500, 501.

and in true faith love him, that we call upon him and are obedient to him as we bear our crosses and throughout our life, that we sincerely love other people, help them charitably, in all peril of life and death put our full confidence in the grace secured for us in Christ, and look forward to living eternally with God.

How longingly the worthy and sainted Dr. Nicholas Selnecker lamented conditions when he wrote in the foreword to his work on the Psalms:[36]

> One constantly finds more and more books that are full of quarreling, disputing, scolding, and reviling, and full of debatable materials which serve no purpose except that of scholastic wrangling. On the other hand, where can one find or buy good books of doctrine and consolation which expound the Word of God plainly and honestly and present pure doctrine well? Such books are supposed to be good things, better than any sacred relics, and yet they are usually filled with personal animus and secret vindictiveness and distortion of truth. If one puts aside books with human thoughts which arise apart from God's Word and Holy Spirit and rejects books which contain unnecessary wrangling and disputation, vindictiveness, personal ambition, and slander, one will surely find only a few books that have been written in our time.

The former Coburg superintendent Master Dinckel agreed with this in his preface to Luther's prayer book,[37] and he also observed the harm that results: "The consequence is that true *theologia practica* (that is, the teaching of faith, love, and hope) is relegated to a secondary place, and the way is again paved for a *theologia spinosa* (that is, a prickly, thorny teaching) which scratches and irritates hearts and souls, as used to happen before Luther's time."

Although these and other well meaning teachers have sincerely lamented such conditions and have hoped for improvement, hardly

---

[36] Nikolaus Selnecker, 1530-1592, *Der gantze Psalter des Königlichen Propheten Davids aussgelegt* (Nürnberg, 1569).

[37] Johannes Dinckel, 1545-1601, put out an edition of Luther's *Betbüchlein*, but no copy of it appears to be extant today.

anything has been accomplished. In fact, it would appear that the evil has increased rather than decreased. At the beginning of this century the sainted and thoughtful Dr. John Valentine Andreae[38] not only earnestly lamented the tendency in many of his writings but also often pricked the rather sensitive skins of persons who were responsible. But *surdis fabulae!*[39]

Thus we learn much that we often wish we had not learned. Meanwhile that is neglected on which everything depends, as we have heard above from Luther's words. How many a Christian minister, when by God's grace he first enters upon his office, has the experience that many of the things to which he devotes hard work and great pains prove to be useless, that he must begin all over again to reflect on what is more necessary, and that he wishes he had known this before and had been wisely and carefully directed to it. Even in our day there is no want of such men who are concerned about the church of God and who observe this defect. It was not without profound feelings (of joy, and then, because there was no fruit, of sadness) that I read what Dr. Balthasar Raith, Christian theologian in Württemberg and my acknowledged and honored patron in the Lord, said in Tübingen in 1669 in his address at the funeral of the late renowned Dr. Zeller:[40] "Several years ago, when he and the sainted Dr. Weller,[41] the theologian who had served the Saxon church well, attended the diet of Regensburg, they deliberated about how the scholastic theology which Luther had thrown out the front door had been introduced again by others through the back door, and how this theology was more recently eliminated once again from the Evangelical church and the

[38] Johann Valentin Andreae, 1586-1654, was the author, among many other books, of *Christianopolis, an Ideal State,* trans. F. E. Held (New York, 1916).

[39] Latin: these are tales for those who will not hear.

[40] *Dominus Christophorus Zellerus . . . suprema laudatione celebratus . . . a Balthasare Raithio* (Tübingen, 1669), p. 17. Christoph Zeller, 1605-1669, was a consistorial councilor and provost in Württemberg. Balthasar Raith, 1616-1683, was professor in Tübingen.

[41] Jakob Weller, 1602-1664, professor in Wittenberg.

true biblical theology put in its place."[42] If God blessed that deliberation of valiant theologians and would bless future deliberations aiming at the same end, it would probably be one of the greatest benefactions for which we could give thanks to the goodness of God.

This defect does more harm than most people imagine, for they become accustomed to those very things about which St. Paul long ago warned his Timothy when he commanded that certain persons should "not occupy themselves with myths and endless genealogies which promote speculations rather than the divine training that is in faith; whereas the aim of our charge is love that issues from a pure heart and a good conscience and sincere faith. Certain persons by swerving from these have wandered away into vain discussion, desiring to be teachers of the law, without understanding either what they are saying or the things about which they make assertions" (I Tim. 1:4-7). Again, St. Paul said in I Timothy 6:3-5: "If anyone teaches otherwise and does not agree with the sound words of our Lord Jesus Christ" (these words are pure simplicity, not human sophistry but divine wisdom) "and the teaching which accords with godliness" (here let us pay attention to the purpose of our studies!), "he is puffed up with conceit" (for he imagines himself to be the most learned master in Israel, who knows everything, and he has the reputation of being just that), "he knows nothing; he has a morbid craving for controversy and for disputes about words, which produce envy, dissension, slander, base suspicions, and wrangling among men who are depraved in mind and bereft of the truth, imagining that godliness is a means of gain." So St. Paul also faithfully warned his Colossians (Col. 2:8): "See to it that no one makes a prey of you by philosophy and empty deceit, according to human tradition, according to the elemental spirits of the universe, and not according to Christ."

[42] The quotation is reproduced in a shorter Latin form as well as in a German rendering.

When men's minds are stuffed with such a theology which, while it preserves the foundation of faith from the Scriptures, builds on it with so much wood, hay, and stubble[43] of human inquisitiveness that the gold can no longer be seen, it becomes exceedingly difficult to grasp and find pleasure in the real simplicity of Christ and his teaching. This is so because men's taste becomes accustomed to the more charming things of reason, and after a while the simplicity of Christ and his teaching appears to be tasteless. Such knowledge, which remains without love, "puffs up" (I Cor. 8:1). It leaves man in his love of self; indeed, it fosters and strengthens such love more and more. Subtleties unknown to the Scriptures usually have their origin, in the case of those who introduce them, in a desire to exhibit their sagacity and their superiority over others, to have a great reputation, and to derive benefit therefrom in the world. Moreover, these subtleties are themselves of such a nature that they stimulate, in those who deal with them, not a true fear of God but a thirst for honor and other impulses which are unbecoming a true Christian. When people are practiced in such things they begin to have great illusions and introduce them at once into the church of Christ, even if they know little or nothing of the one thing needful, which they hold in little esteem. They can hardly be kept from taking to market what gives them the most pleasure, and they generally concentrate on something that is not very edifying to their hearers who are seeking salvation. When they really achieve the purpose they set themselves, they succeed in giving those of their hearers who have ready minds a fair knowledge of religious controversies, and these hearers regard it as the greatest honor to dispute with others. Both preachers and hearers confine themselves to the notion that the one thing needful is the assertion and retention of pure doctrine, which must not be overthrown by errors, even if it is very much obscured with human perversions.

[43] Cf. I Cor. 3:12.

How, then, can one do anything but repeat the appeal of St. Paul in I Corinthians 2:4-5? "My speech and my message were not in plausible words of wisdom, but in demonstration of the Spirit and power, that your faith might not rest in the wisdom of men but in the power of God." Indeed, we may say that the highly enlightened apostle, if he came among us today, would probably understand only a little of what our slippery geniuses sometimes say in holy places. This means that he derived his knowledge not from human ingenuity but from the illumination of the Spirit, and these are as far removed from each other as heaven is from earth. As little as divine illumination can be grasped by human ingenuity, so little can souls filled with divine illumination comfortably stoop to the feeble fantasies of human ingenuity.

[Defects in the Common People]

Since conditions are such in the first two estates, which ought to govern the masses and lead them to godliness, it is easy to guess how things are in the third estate. Indeed, it is evident on every hand that none of the precepts of Christ is openly observed. Our dear Savior long ago gave us the mark of distinction, "By this all men will know that you are my disciples, if you have love for one another" (John 13:35). Here love is considered the distinguishing mark, and this is not merely a pretended love that is hugged to one's heart in unfruitful embrace but a love that manifests itself openly. I John 3:18 ["Let us not love in word or speech but in deed and in truth"]. If we judge by this mark, how difficult it will be to find even a small number of real and true disciples of Christ among the great mass of nominal Christians! Nevertheless, the word of the Lord does not deceive but remains true now and forever.

When one looks at the everyday life even of those among us who are called Lutherans (but who do not deserve this name, for they do not understand dear Luther's teaching about living faith), does one not find grave offense—indeed, such offenses as are everywhere prevalent? I shall not say vices which the world, too, acknowledges to be wrong, for ultimately such offense does not do so much harm. Much graver is the injury that comes from sins which are no longer recognized as sins or whose gravity is no longer realized.

We must confess that *drunkenness* is to be counted among such sins. It is not only prevalent in high and low places, among persons of the ecclesiastical and political estates, but also has its defenders among those who, while conceding that people who make a business of getting drunk are guilty of sin, nevertheless wish to maintain that it is no sin, or at least no sin worth mentioning, to drink occasionally (as long as it does not happen too often) to a good friend's health. Consequently, this sin is never penitently acknowledged, for if it were acknowledged, one would develop such a hatred for it that one would never again drink to another's health. But who among the common people does not deem it strange and preposterous that this sin, too, must once and for all be renounced if they are to be children of God? Such people are more likely to think that those who declaim against this sin must be peculiar individuals or must have other reasons for their hostility to this pleasant diversion than a recognition that their teaching on this matter is divine. And it is divine, for St. Paul in I Corinthians 6:9-10 regards drunkards as belonging to no better company (before God) than whores, idolaters, adulterers, homosexuals, thieves, the greedy, revilers, and robbers, all of whom are excluded by him from the kingdom of God.

Here the excuse is not valid that a distinction must be made between the man who drinks all the time and seeks his own pleasure in drinking and others who drink seldom, on eventful occasions, and to the health of others, as if St. Paul meant the former and not the latter. Although the validity of this objection can be denied on the basis of other passages of the Scriptures, I wish simply to ask such people if they regard as damnable the life of only those who practice whoredom every day, commit adultery every day, engage in homosexual relations, steal, rob, etc. every day, or if they do not consider it too much to do these things even once a year, not to say once a month, and if they do not believe that unless such sins are earnestly and resolutely rooted out these vicious and unrepentant persons will lose their salvation. Although everybody who has some knowledge of God will, I suppose, acknowledge this, how is it that we pay so little attention to this one sin of drunkenness and are hardly willing to consider it culpable unless it occurs frequently? What can we advance in defense of it except that it is an ancient inherited custom of Germans and Scandinavians which is abetted by the temperament of some of them? Are we to say, however, that this custom makes the Word of God of no effect? Surely as little as Paul's assertion to the Corinthians could reasonably have been opposed on the ground that such a custom had also taken hold among the Greeks. Just as we cannot minimize the particular vices of other nations, which may be addicted to lechery, stealing, or the like, so they cannot excuse us on account of our drunkenness. Even less will the just God allow us to abolish his law.

If some advance the argument that drunkenness cannot be so grave a sin because, if it were, there would be very few true Christians among us, I shall accept the conclusion and add that this sin is all the more dangerous because it has spread so widely and is recognized by so few, with the result that, like those in Sodom,[44] our people boast of their drunkenness or gloss over it or regard it as a peccadillo.

Let us also look at the general practice of *lawsuits*. If they are properly examined one must confess that it is rather rare for a suit to be conducted by either side in such a way as not to violate

[44] Cf. Isa. 3:9; Gen. 19:1-14.

or go beyond the bounds of Christian love. Although it is not wrong to make use of the divine assistance in civil authority and seek it in judicial procedure, in such a suit we must do everything for our neighbor which we expect others to do for us.[45] That this does not happen as a rule and that most litigants use the courts as instruments of their vindictiveness, injustice, and unseemly cupidity is also a sin which is not considered a sin and is therefore seldom mentioned in the confession of sins.

If we look at trade, the crafts, and other occupations through which men seek to earn their living, we shall find that everything is not arranged according to the precepts of Christ but rather that not a few public regulations and traditional usages in these occupations are diametrically opposed to them. Where is there anybody who remembers that not only his own support and gain (to which almost all attention is directed) but also the glory of his God and the welfare of his neighbor should be the object of all that he does in his station in life? Thus it happens that it is not accounted a sin to employ tricks which do not have an evil reputation in the world but are rather praised as shrewd and circumspect measures, even if they are burdensome to our neighbors and, indeed, oppress and impoverish them. The very ones who mean to be the best Christians have no scruples about such tricks. Wretched custom has obscured the precepts of Christianity to such an extent that we think it absurd when in a given instance somebody practices what is acknowledged by all, namely, that we should love our neighbor as ourselves,[46] although the force of these words is little pondered.

Although the community which the Christians established in the early Jerusalem church was not commanded,[47] who considers that perhaps another kind of *community of goods* may be very

[45] Cf. Matt. 7:12.
[46] Cf. Matt. 22:39.
[47] Cf. Acts 2:44-45; 4:32-37.

necessary? Since I must acknowledge that I have nothing which is my own, but that everything belongs to God, and I am appointed to be a steward over it, I am not at all free to keep what is mine when and as long as I please. On the contrary, when I see that, for the honor of the householder and the need of my fellow servants, love demands that I use what is mine, I must not hesitate to offer it as community property which, to be sure, my neighbor cannot demand by civil right but which, according to the divine right of love, I dare not withhold and keep to myself as long as my neighbor's needs cannot be met in another way. Are not these, when one mentions them, regarded as strange teachings? Yet they are a necessary consequence of Christian love and were manifested throughout the primitive church, so that neither did complete community of goods, in which nobody possesses anything of his own, put an end to opportunity for virtue and Christian love, nor did worldly property present an impediment to brotherly love.

Among the earliest Christians, therefore, the rich had no advantage other than that they had to be rich also in good deeds (I Tim. 6:18) and that they took the trouble and pains to manage the property which they were ready at any moment to use wherever they saw need and they could bear witness to their love of God and neighbor. The poor bore no other burden (if this is to be regarded as a burden) than that they lived not by their own hands but with the aid of their brethren. There was no need of begging among the brethren, and its appearance would surely have been considered unbecoming, even as God was unwilling to permit it in his well framed form of government for the Jews in the Old Testament (Deut. 15:4). Now, however, things have come to such a pass that not only is begging very common—and it is to be looked upon as a means, encouragement, and cloak of many terrible sins, a hardship to those who are really needy, a dangerous defect of the common weal for persons disposed to Christian charity, and indeed a blot on our Christianity—but most people hardly know any other way of helping a needy neighbor than reluctantly to toss a few pennies to a beggar once in a while. They are far from recognizing that they are obligated to perform such deeds of love even when their own livelihood may be noticeably affected by their gifts. While by divine decree the people of the Old Testament had to lay aside and give more than a tenth (for there were several kinds of tithe, as may be seen from the law)[48] for the support of the ministry, the service of God, and the poor, we do not consider that the benefactions which have been bestowed on us by Christ, and which are greater than those which the people of the Old Testament received, obligate us, when the need of a neighbor demands it, to be ready to give not less but more and, in fact, all that we possess. That this does not happen, and that the charity of most of the people who mean to be benevolent almost never goes beyond contributing "out of their abundance" (Mark 12:44), is a rather clear indication that we are so far from a sincere practice of real brotherly love that we can hardly believe what it requires.

This is not the place to specify everything. These examples will suffice to illustrate that such sins are prevalent among us. To be sure, they are not regarded as sins (although they are contrary to our duties as these are described in the Scriptures) and their offense is so much the greater.

We must go beyond this and see how the great mass of people thinks about *the service of God*. It is not in accord with our salutary teaching as the sainted Dr. Paulus Tarnovius set it forth so wonderfully in his address on the new gospel,[49] which discloses how well this zealous man perceived what is wanting and which therefore deserves to be widely read.

---

[48] Cf. Lev. 27:30-33; Num. 18:21-24; Deut. 14:22-27, 26:12-15.

[49] Paul Tarnov, *De novo evangelio quod sit causa omnium calamitatum . . .* (Frankfurt, 1697). The address of Tarnov, 1562-1633, was delivered in Rostock in 1624, and Spener often appealed to it to show that his own teaching was not new.

We gladly acknowledge that we must be saved only and alone through faith and that our works or godly life contribute neither much nor little to our salvation, for as a fruit of our faith our works are connected with the gratitude which we owe to God, who has already given us who believe the gift of righteousness and salvation. Far be it from us to depart even a finger's breadth from this teaching, for we would rather give up our life and the whole world than yield the smallest part of it.

We also gladly acknowledge the power of the Word of God when it is preached, since it is the power of God for salvation to everyone who has faith (Rom. 1:16). We are bound diligently to hear the Word of God not only because we are commanded to do so but also because it is the divine hand which offers and presents grace to the believer, whom the Word itself awakens through the Holy Spirit.

Nor do I know how to praise Baptism and its power highly enough. I believe that it is the real "washing of regeneration and renewal in the Holy Spirit" (Tit. 3:5), or as Luther says in the Catechism, "it effects forgiveness of sins, delivers from death and the devil, and grants" (not merely promises) "eternal salvation."[50]

Not less gladly do I acknowledge the glorious power in the sacramental, oral, and not merely spiritual eating and drinking[51] of the body and blood of the Lord in the Holy Supper. On this account I heartily reject the position of the Reformed when they deny that we receive such a pledge of our salvation in, with, and under the bread and wine, when they weaken its power, and when they see in it no more than exists outside the holy sacrament in spiritual eating and drinking.

While I adhere with all my heart to every one of these teachings of our church and bear witness to them with my lips, and

[50] Luther's *Small Catechism*, IV, 6.

[51] Most Lutherans held that John 6:25-65 referred to spiritual eating and drinking, not to actual eating and drinking, and therefore not to the sacrament.

PIA DESIDERIA

find more pleasure in the writings of Luther than in any other author precisely because there is more of these teachings there, I cannot deny that the great mass of people, who also call themselves Evangelical, have other opinions and notions of the matter which are contrary to our teaching and the confession of the church.

How many there are who live such a manifestly unchristian life that they themselves cannot deny that the law is broken at every point, who have no intention of mending their ways in the future, and yet who pretend to be firmly convinced that they will be saved in spite of all this! If one asks on what they base their expectation one will discover, as they themselves confess, that they are sure of this because it is of course not possible to be saved on account of one's life, but that they believe in Christ and put all their trust in him, that this cannot fail, and that they will surely be saved by such faith. Accordingly they have a fleshly illusion of faith (for godly faith does not exist without the Holy Spirit, nor can such faith continue when deliberate sins prevail) in place of the faith that saves. This is a delusion of the devil, as terrible as any error ever has been or can be, to ascribe salvation to such a fancy of secure man. How differently does our dear Luther speak of faith! In his preface to the Epistle to the Romans he wrote:[52]

Faith is not that human notion and dream that some hold for faith. Because they see that no betterment of life and no good works follow it, and yet they can hear and say much about faith, they fall into error and say, "Faith is not enough; one must do works in order to be righteous and be saved." This is the reason why, when they hear the gospel, they go ahead and by their own powers fashion an idea in their hearts which says, "I believe." This they hold for true faith. But it is a human imagination and idea that never reaches the depths of the heart, and so nothing comes of it and no betterment

[52] WA, DB, 7, pp. 9, 10. English in Works of Martin Luther (hereafter referred to as WML) (6 vols., Philadelphia: A. J. Holman Co., 1915-1932), 6, 451, 452, and in Luther's Works (hereafter referred to as LW) (55 vols., Philadelphia and St. Louis, 1955-   ), 35, 370.

64

follows it. Faith, however, is a divine work in us. It changes us and makes us to be born anew of God (John 1:13). It kills the old Adam and makes altogether different men of us in heart and spirit and mind and powers, and it brings with it the Holy Spirit. O, it is a living, busy, active, mighty thing, this faith, and so it is impossible for it not to do good works incessantly. It does not ask whether there are good works to do, but before the question rises it has already done them and is always at the doing of them, etc.

I shall not quote other passages in which Luther wrote in the same vein. Read especially in his *Church Postil,* summer festival season, folio 65a,[53] where he describes divine and human faith very forcefully and distinguishes one from the other. So it is that all those who live under the rule of sin, with the consequence that they have no capacity for the Holy Spirit and hence for true faith, can have no other kind of faith than such human delusion. How great, alas, is the number of these!

Just as the above illusion of faith as the only means of salvation from our side does great harm, so from the side of the divine means of Word and sacraments the shameful illusion of an *opus operatum*[54] is added. This is not less harmful to the church, leads many people to damnation, and strengthens the aforementioned false notion of what true faith is. We cannot deny—on the contrary, daily experience convinces us—that there are not a few who think that all that Christianity requires of them (and that having done this, they have done quite enough in their service of God) is that they be baptized, hear the preaching of God's Word, confess and receive absolution, and go to the Lord's Supper, no matter how their hearts are disposed at the time, whether or not there are fruits which follow, provided they at least live in such a way that the civil authorities do not find them liable to punishment. The

[53] Later, in 1700, Spener himself prepared for the press an edition of Luther's *Kirchenpostille.* See *WA,* 22.

[54] Latin: the mere outward performance of an act. How Spener understood this is made clear in what follows.

illusion of these people is described by John Arndt in his *True Christianity*:[55] "I am baptized into Christ, I have the pure Word of God and hear it, I receive the sacrament of the Lord's Supper, and I also believe and confess all the articles of the Christian faith. Therefore I cannot be lacking in anything, my actions must be pleasing to God, and I am in the right way to be saved. This, alas, is the false reasoning of many in this day who regard their outward performance as constituting true righteousness." See the answer which John Arndt gives in the same place.[56]

Thereby these blind people turn the holy intention of God upside down. Your God has indeed given you Baptism, and you may be baptized only once. But he has made a covenant with you—from his side a covenant of grace and from your side a covenant of faith and a good conscience. This covenant must last through your whole life. It will be in vain that you comfort yourself in your Baptism and in its promise of grace and salvation if for your part you do not also remain in the covenant of faith and a good conscience or, having departed therefrom, return to it with sincere repentance. Accordingly if your Baptism is to benefit you, it must remain in constant use throughout your life.

Again, you hear the Word of God. This is good. But it is not enough that your ear hears it. Do you let it penetrate inwardly into your heart and allow the heavenly food to be digested there, so that you get the benefit of its vitality and power, or does it go in one ear and out the other? If the former, then the words of the Lord in Luke 11:28 apply to you: "Blessed are those who hear the word of God and keep it." If the latter, then the work of hearing will not save you but rather increase your condemnation because you have not made better use of the grace you received. How many there are, alas, who cannot say of themselves

---

[55] Johann Arndt, *Wahres Christenthum*, II, iv, 3. John Arndt, *True Christianity*, trans. A. W. Boehm and Charles F. Schaeffer (Philadelphia, 1868), p. 175.

[56] *Ibid.*, pp. 175-177.

that they have let God's Word bear fruit in them and yet think that, in their view, they have so obeyed and served God that he must save them!

This is also true of confession and absolution, which we hold to be an effective means of evangelical comfort and the forgiveness of sins. It is this, however, to none but believers. Why is it, then, that so many, who do not have the slightest bit of that aforementioned true faith, confess and have themselves absolved even while they remain unrepentant, as if their confession and absolution would be of benefit to them simply because they have performed an act, spoken a confession, and received an absolution?

The same is the case with the Lord's Supper. There are extraordinarily many people who think only of discharging this holy work and of how often they do it. But they hardly consider whether their spiritual life may be strengthened thereby, whether they proclaim the Lord's death with their hearts, lips, and life, whether the Lord works in and rules over them or they have left the old Adam on his throne. This can only mean that the dangerous error of the *opus operatum,* for which we condemn the papists, has in some measure been reintroduced without our really being aware of it.

The teaching of our church is not to blame for any of this, for it vigorously opposes such illusions. Rather is it the wickedness of men and the craftiness of the devil which seek to make of the divine means of grace occasions for greater security and accordingly of greater condemnation. Besides, it is not to be denied that some preachers ought to protest more diligently against such security and false notions in order to open the eyes of the people, for many could thus be awakened out of their sleep and snatched from destruction.

Although our Evangelical Lutheran church is a true church and is pure in its teaching, it is in such a condition, unfortunately, that we behold its outward form with sorrowful eyes.

[Offenses Resulting from these Defects]

The Jews who live among us are the first to be offended by all this. They are strengthened in their unbelief and, indeed, are moved to blaspheme the name of the Lord. They cannot believe it possible that we hold that Christ is true God because we do not obey his commands, or they conclude that Jesus must have been a wicked man when they judge him and his teaching by our lives. We cannot deny that the offense which we have given these poor people has been a major cause of the past hardheartedness of the Jews and a major impediment to their conversion. This was vigorously deplored, among others, by the late Dr. John George Dorsch, well-known professor in Strasbourg and afterwards in Rostock, when he responded in this way to Mr. Jacob Helwig's inaugural disputation[57] on the apostolic mystery in Romans 11:25, 26:

> Just as the Jews, insofar as they were able to do so, once prohibited the proclamation of the Gospel to the Gentiles, so the Christians today not only throw away their own salvation but also hinder the salvation of Jews and other unbelievers (which they ought to promote and bring about) by the most harmful offenses, such as impiety, hypocrisy, injustice, frauds, unchastity, and other shameful acts, schisms, hatred, strife, monstrous and cruel wars, and (what is the chief thing) the sad tearing and breaking asunder of the bonds of holy, brotherly love. Since such things, which can never be reconciled with saving faith, are so prevalent among us, who will not bitterly bewail the corrupt, dangerous, and almost desperate condition of our churches? Who will doubt that ours are the last days, whose times are hard to bear? Who will not include most of the people who profess the name of Christ in the number of those who are to be cut off by God's severe judgment on account of their unbelief? For what else is the dissolute and ungodly life of today's Christians (who

---

[57] *Dissertatio inauguralis de mysterio apostolico divino Rom. XI, v. 25, 26* (Rostock, 1658). Helwig, 1631-1684, was rector in Berlin, German pastor in Stockholm, bishop of Estonia, and president of the consistory in Reval (Tallinn). Spener reproduces the quotation in Latin and then provides a German translation.

simulate the form of piety but deny the power thereof, and who through an abuse of the longsuffering and goodness of God heap up wrath as a treasure) but a testimony and public witness to their wickedness and unbelief?

In addition to the Jews, all sorts of heretics are offended by us. Chief among these are papists, who in their hostility toward us never stop boasting, as if the life of our Christians were a fruit of the teaching of the gospel and of the Reformation of Luther. Although their charges, which have been made in published writings, have long since been refuted by godly ministers (even as my beloved friend and brother in the Lord, Dr. William Zesch, recently stopped the mouth of an adversary in the second part of his defense against Father Sevenstern, cap. 5, art. 2, p. 290),[58] they do not cease repeating them again and again, confusing the weak among us with their insinuations and strengthening their own adherents in their loathing of our religion.

Besides, there are many others, including some well disposed individuals, who arrive at the conclusion: We are stuck fast in Babel as much as the Roman church is, and therefore we cannot boast of our withdrawal from it.

Above all, it is known only to God with what sorrow godly people behold these distressing conditions and with how many thousands of sighs and tears they lament the ruin of Joseph,[59] for they see the conditions with their own eyes, can foresee no improvement in them, and in fact observe that they are constantly becoming worse. How often do they borrow the words of their beloved David in Psalm 119? "Hot indignation seizes me because of the wicked, who forsake thy law" (v. 53). "My eyes shed streams

---

[58] Wilhelm Zesch, *Einfältige Antwort auf die fürgelegte Glaubens-frag: Ob die Evangelische . . . Kirche . . . sey die wahre Apostolisch-Catholisch oder Christliche Kirche . . . verteidiget wider P. Casparum Sevenstern der Jesuitischen Societät Priestern* (Frankfurt, 1673). Zesch, 1629-1682, was superintendent in Wertheim.

[59] Cf. Amos 6:6.

of tears because men do not keep thy law" (v. 136). "My zeal consumes me because my foes forget thy words" (v. 139). "I look at the faithless with disgust because they do not keep thy commands" (v. 158), etc. The more sincerely such godly people love God and the more they desire to see advance in the hallowing of his name, the extension of his kingdom, and the doing of his will—all of which they pray for daily—the more it pains them to see such abominations. They grieve over the many souls they know to be in such danger. It is hard for them to keep themselves unspotted from the world amid such scandals, and they worry lest, if not they, at least their children may in time be seduced and carried away on the tide of evil. Those who by God's blessing live in outward tranquillity and wealth do not enjoy their circumstances because they are dismayed by the general wretchedness. If they were not supported by the strong hand of God and if they were not thereby given assurance (even if they themselves would not live to experience a general improvement) that God would give them their lives as a prize of war (as he did Baruch, Jer. 45:5), they would drown in their sorrow.

This tragic situation, meanwhile, is the chief thing that prevents many well-disposed individuals who are still in other and heterodox churches, especially Roman churches, and who are fairly well aware of this abomination, from uniting with us, as they would have done in former times. Although this may seem unbelievable, there are some people, outwardly connected with the Roman church, who really think of the pope and his see as the antichrist prophesied by God and whose hearts may sometimes be perceived to pour forth sorrowful laments. Although they recognize some errors in their own church and not only errors but also abominations in other churches, and would therefore be willing, if only they could find a real and palpable church of Christ, joyfully to unite with it, they finally come to the conclusion that there no longer is any pure church on earth, that the children of God are still captives in Babylon, that they must consequently await the redemption of God with patience, and that in this Babylonian captivity they must serve God, insofar as possible, with fear and trembling, meanwhile abstaining from the grossest vices and bewailing the rest. They know no other solution, and so they live in constant unrest and anxiety. Because they look at our church only as it appears to the outward eye, inasmuch as most of them are unacquainted with our teaching (and those who are acquainted with it regard doctrine which does not regulate life as mere pretense and expect to discern the kingdom of God not in words but in power), they hold that our church is the true church as little as their own, that everything is a Babylonian hodge-podge, one part of which is almost as bad as another, and that it is consequently not worth transferring from one church to another.

To be sure, these people cannot be excused, for they have opportunity enough to become familiar with the teaching of our church. Moreover, if they should find that our teaching agrees with the Word of God, and theirs is in conflict with it, they would be bound in conscience to unite with the church which is pure at least in doctrine and where they can be assured (according to the divine promise in Isaiah 55:3) that they would encounter true and godly children of God, where they would acquiesce in no error when they confess their faith, where they would not be compelled to participate in any idolatry or like sins during public worship, and where they could keep themselves clean despite the many offensive things they would have to see.

It would indeed be going entirely too far to identify our church with Babel on account of the offenses which have been mentioned. What the spiritual Babel is we must learn from the Holy Spirit alone. Through John's pen he has described it in Revelation 18:5, 9, 18 in such a way that one ought to be able to discover it with half-closed eyes. It can be nothing but Rome, the great city which had imperial power over the kings of the earth, and this with spiritual rule, for after losing its worldly rule over the earth it sought power again in spiritual rule. Beyond this we do not have the power to enlarge upon the spiritual Babel according to our own whim without the guidance of the Scriptures. Accordingly no church can belong to Babel if it openly repudiates Babel and its rule and does not submit in the least to its will or allow itself to be governed by it, even if it may have shortcomings and something of the evil practices which are characteristic of Babel.

We cannot sufficiently thank God for leading us by the blessed work of the Reformation out of the Babylonian captivity of Rome (as the Jews were once led out by the decree of Cyrus under the high priest Joshua and Prince Zerubbabel)[60] and setting us down in blessed freedom. Something of what once happened to the Jews, however, also happened to us. The Jews had indeed returned, they occupied city and land, they began to build, and by the second year they had laid the foundation for the house of the Lord. But there were disagreeable people who stood in the way, and an adverse command was received from King Artaxerxes that the building should stop until the second year of King Darius.[61] To this was added the great remissness of the Jews, who were content to have been liberated from Babel and to be able to have some of their religious services again. They were not eager to restore the services to good condition but simply enjoyed their temporal peace and tranquillity. The Lord called to them through Haggai: "This people say the time is not yet come to rebuild the house of the Lord. . . . Is it a time for you yourselves to dwell in your paneled houses while this house lies in ruins?" (Hag. 1:2, 4). Although the Jews were no longer in captivity, their spiritual and temporal condition was not at all what it ought to be, and the contempt for the house of the Lord which they had become accustomed to in Babylon was strongly adhered to, so that their spiritual condition was perhaps

[60] Cf. II Chron. 36:22-23 Ezra 1-3.
[61] Cf. Ezra 4.

not much better than it had been in captivity. Finally, through the earnest admonition of the prophets Haggai and Zechariah, the temple was completed under the supervision of Zerubbabel and Joshua.[62] This does not mean that everything was done that ought to have been done, nor was everything restored that had before been destroyed by the king of Babylon. Ezra, the scribe, came, to be followed after some years by Nehemiah, and these men did much to reorganize the church, rebuild the walls of the city, and restore civil government. The books of Ezra and Nehemiah, which record all this, should be read, for much will be found there that applies to our time.

Just as it may not be concluded that the Jews were still in their Babylonian captivity because their affairs in Jerusalem were not in the condition in which they ought to be, so it does not follow that we may today be returned to Babel, on account of the shortcomings in our condition, by those who are ungrateful for God's blessing in the Reformation. It was not enough for the Jews to leave their Babylonian exile; they were expected to restore the temple and its beautiful services. So we, too, ought not to be satisfied with the knowledge that we have gone out of Babel but we ought to take pains to correct the defects which still remain.

This is precisely what the complaints of godly people are aimed at when they lament our wretched condition, namely, that we should encourage one another and promote the work of the Lord ever more earnestly than before. The objection raised by some that we should not uncover the failings and disgrace of the church, so that our adversaries may not become aware of them but that they remain concealed, is to be answered by saying that it would be irresponsible to expose such infirmities to the world merely to gloat over them. A Ham or a Canaan who looks upon the nakedness of his father Noah with pleasure and derision will be struck with a

[62] Cf. Hag. 1:7-15; Ezra 5:1-2.

curse.[63] But the complaints of the godly, as the Searcher of hearts knows, proceed from a different motive and purpose. It is out of a fervent love and zeal for God's glory that we lament what is in conflict with this cause and that we desire to move one individual or another to take an earnest interest in it. It is a love which causes me to uncover dangerous injuries in order to show them to persons who might be expected to heal them.

Besides, we are not uncovering anything that is not, unfortunately, already generally known. It is not our intention to mention any of the more secret defects of the church. Such of these as concern our adversaries, however, it would be vain to try to conceal from them. If we think that they ought to be kept secret on account of our adversaries, we flatter ourselves to suppose that they do not see these things more clearly than we do. Our enemies have lynx eyes and see many things which we are not ourselves aware of. Consequently if we try to conceal what our adversaries have long since observed, we shall achieve nothing except to be reproached with more justice afterwards when we try in some fashion to defend our situation. On the other hand, if we acknowledge our faults and express our hearty displeasure over them, it will be more manifest that the *whole* church is not to blame. In fact, when our adversaries come to look upon the imperfections in such a way as to realize that they do not ensue from our religion itself but that the hearts of men are altogether tainted, we can best demonstrate that the infirmity inheres in the members or the externals by exposing it without reservation. In any case, our adversaries—the Roman church in particular—cannot use to their advantage the external imperfections which we ourselves confess. Not to mention those atrocities and crimes of theirs which have been exhibited to the world by our side, honest people and well-disposed men among their own children, whether in the spiritual or the secular estate,

[63] Cf. Gen. 9:20-27.

both recently and in earlier times, have upbraided and still daily upbraid them for similar faults. This they cannot deny. They must rather be ashamed of their own weaknesses. They must therefore sweep the dirt from their own door before they boast that things are not so clean as they might be elsewhere. The fact of the matter is that many of the bad things which are found among us can rightfully be laid at the doorstep of the Roman church on the ground that we have inherited them and that similar, additional, and even worse things still prevail among them.

Meanwhile we should be urged on by our love of the church and the glory of God to make improvements, fulfill the longings of godly people, and open wide to the erring the gates to a knowledge of the truth. To such an end we must be careful to examine diligently all the failings in our church and, since our adversaries are themselves sufficiently aware of them without our pointing them out, not be the only ones to shut our eyes to our shortcomings. Suffice it to say that whoever is the Lord's must, to the best of his ability, lend a helping hand, as in a common cause.

[PART II]

[THE POSSIBILITY OF BETTER CONDITIONS IN THE CHURCH]

If we consult the Holy Scriptures we can have no doubt that God promised his church here on earth a better state than this.

In the first place, we have the glorious prophecy of St. Paul and the mystery revealed by him in Romans 11:25-26, that after the full number of the Gentiles comes in, all Israel will be saved. So if not all, at least a perceptibly large number of Jews who have hitherto hardened their hearts will be converted to the Lord. When properly understood, many passages of the Old Testament prophets, like Hosea 3:4-5, will also be seen to refer to the same thing. In addition to the ancient church fathers, probably the most prominent of our own theologians have professed the mystery in the aforementioned passage of Paul. It is to be conceded, however, that besides our otherwise esteemed teacher Dr. Luther, some other prominent doctors of ours have ventured to question whether Paul meant to say what the passage literally asserts; they maintain that the prophecy has been sufficiently fulfilled by the conversion of Jews since the time of the apostles. While on the one hand we do not intend to combat this opinion with extensive arguments or to reproach those who have held it (for we know very well that before a prophecy is fulfilled it may easily happen that enlightened people of good understanding may misinterpret it), on the other hand we

76

do not wish to be diverted from the literal meaning, with which the whole context of Paul's letter harmonizes wonderfully. We trust that nobody will take this amiss.

In the second place, we can expect a great fall in papal Rome. Although Rome was given a decided jolt by the blessed Martin Luther, its spiritual power is still too great to permit us to claim that the prophecy in Revelation 18 and 19 has been completely fulfilled, especially when one observes with what emphatic words the fulfillment is described by the Holy Spirit in those chapters.

If these two things happen, I do not see how anybody can doubt that the whole true church would be in a more glorious and blessed condition than it is now. In order for the Jews to be converted, the true church must be in a holier state than now if its holy life is to be a means for that conversion, or at least the impediments to such conversion (which, as we have seen above, have hitherto consisted of offenses) are to be removed. On the other hand, if the Jews are converted by God's power in a manner which it is impossible for us to foresee, it is unthinkable that the example of this newly converted people (who would undoubtedly have a zeal like that of the early heathen who were converted to Christianity) would not be followed by a remarkable change and improvement in our church. It is to be hoped in any event that the whole church of God, made up of Jews and heathen, would with mutual emulation serve God in one faith and its rich fruits and with holy zeal edify all its members.

Much would be contributed to this end not only if the scandal of anti-Christian Rome were done away with but also if those who are now living under its grievous tyranny and (like those who lived before Luther's time) are sighing yearningly for salvation without knowing where else to turn (of whom there are some now and again, especially in monasteries) were freed from their bonds and were joyfully led to the freedom of the gospel, which would shine more brightly in their eyes.

Since this has been promised to us by God, the fulfillment of the promise must necessarily follow in its time, inasmuch as not a single word of the Lord will fall to the ground and remain without fruit. While hoping for such fruit, however, it is not enough idly to wait for it and be killed by the desire, as Solomon says of the sluggard,[1] but it is incumbent on all of us to see to it that as much as possible is done, on the one hand, to convert the Jews and weaken the spiritual power of the papacy and, on the other hand, to reform our church. Even if it may be evident that we cannot achieve the whole and complete purpose, we can at least do as much as possible.

There is no doubt at all that the counsel of God will be accomplished without us, and what is revealed in the Scriptures will be fulfilled no matter what we may do. But we should remember that the answer which Mordecai returned to his kinswoman Esther also applies to us: "If you keep silence at such a time as this, relief and deliverance will rise for the Jews from another quarter, but you and your father's house will perish" (Esther 4:14). If we, to whom God restored the bright light of the gospel through his servant Luther, fail to do our duty, God will get help elsewhere and preserve his honor. We must fear, however, that he will punish us grievously for our negligence by depriving us of this light and going to others with it, especially because we have already deserved such punishment a thousand times on account of our great ingratitude. In this connection I cannot refrain from quoting the grieving lament which that excellent theologian Erasmus Sarcerius, who knew more about the welfare of the church than most, wrote in his book on the ways and means of promoting and preserving real and true religion, folio 344:[2]

---

[1] Prov. 21:25.

[2] Erasmus Sarcerius, *Von mitteln und wegen, die rechte und wahre Religion . . . zu befördern und zu erhalten* (1554). At the time when this work was published, Sarcerius, 1501-1559, was superintendent in Eisleben.

Where the Word of God is neglected, real and true religion collapses. Where this collapses, no one can or will be saved. If our sins, our reckless and godless shame, our secure and knavish life, our wickedness and wantonness are compared with the misdeeds of the Jews and our ancestors, I think that we shall not be far apart. It is my considered opinion and judgment that it is not possible for real and true religion to survive amid our devilish, epicurean, and sardanapalian living.[3] Is it not a pity that we blind and callous Germans should with our dissolute and disorderly life have driven out real and true religion? There is no stopping it. Nobody thinks of bettering himself. To sin is human, but to be unwilling to bear the punishment for sin is of the devil. There is still hope if, when one sins, one can bear the punishment for it. Accordingly I conclude that real and true religion has had its day. I fear that when the gospel is still preached it is as a testimony and not for reform. Christ said in Matthew 24:14 that in the last days (and it was of our days that he spoke) the gospel would be preached 'as a testimony.' Even if that comes to pass which Christ also prophesied (when the Son of man comes, will he find faith on the earth?), nobody will pay any attention to decency and discipline. It will happen (God have mercy!) that although each of us poor preachers will teach and cry out, 'Repent and be converted,' everybody will do just as he pleases. Governing authorities do nothing about discipline, and their subjects do not want it. Some faithful preachers wish to restore it, but this is not possible amid such confused and disorderly living. They must do their best and not give up the cause. It is a case of helping wherever possible. Now, as we are concerned about real and true religion, so we also give thought to ways and means of maintaining it. I have no counsel to offer. If I knew what to suggest, nobody would pay any heed. It remains to see with my own eyes, and perhaps I shall experience it without my desiring it, that on account of our sins and transgressions our dear religion will be lost through God's disfavor, even as it once came to us through God's favor.

More than a hundred years ago this dear man was worried that such a thing might happen. Since there has been no improvement

---

[3] Sardanapalus, according to classical myth, was an Assyrian king who burned himself on a pyre with his favorite concubine.

in the meantime, we do not have less reason to worry, for wrath has only multiplied in the meantime. Perhaps we shall be the occasion for the conversion of others, and so we have good reason not to be secure, to be watchful of ourselves, and not to neglect anything in order that our church may be lifted to a different and better condition.

Let no one think that we here intend and seek too much. We are not living in a Platonic state,[4] and so it is not possible to have everything perfect and according to rule. The evil circumstances of our time are therefore to be borne with compassion rather than bewailed with anger. If one seeks perfection one must leave this world and enter the world to come. Only there will one encounter something perfect; one cannot hope for it before then. To those who raise this kind of objection I reply thus: First, we are not forbidden to seek perfection, but we are urged on toward it. And how desirable it would be if we were to achieve it! Second, I cheerfully concede that here in this life we shall not manage that, for the farther a godly Christian advances, the more he will see that he lacks, and so he will never be farther removed from the illusion of perfection than when he tries hardest to reach it.

It is like the observation that as a rule those who have made the most progress in their studies are far less likely to consider themselves learned than others who have just begun to look into books a half-year ago. With the passing of time the former come to a fuller understanding of what true erudition means than they could have had before. So in spiritual matters, too, there is more cause to be concerned about beginners who think themselves to be perfect than about those who have already taken some steps in that direction. Meanwhile, even if we shall never in this life achieve such a degree of perfection that nothing could or should be added, we are nevertheless under obligation to achieve some degree of perfection. What Paul said to the early Christians applies to all Chris-

[4] That is, in an ideal state.

tians: "Finally, brethren, farewell. Be perfect" (II Cor. 13:11). "This also we wish, even your perfection" (v. 9). "We preach, warning every man, and teaching every man in all wisdom, that we may present every man perfect in Christ Jesus" (Col. 1:28). "That the man of God may be perfect, thoroughly furnished unto all good works" (II Tim. 3:17). "Let us therefore, as many as be perfect, be thus minded" (Phil. 3:15), although just before this, in verse 12, Paul said with reference to a higher and here impossible degree of perfection, "Not as though I had already attained, either were already perfect." We may say, then, that the injunctions to become more and more perfect apply to the whole church, and what Paul says in another place should become true of each and every individual: "Till we all come in the unity of the faith and of the knowledge of the Son of God, unto a perfect man, unto the measure of the stature of the fulness of Christ" (Eph. 4:13).[5]

We do not understand the perfection which we demand of the church in such a way that not a single hypocrite is any longer to be found in it, for we know that there is no field of grain in which there are no weeds. What we mean is that the church should be free of manifest offenses, that nobody who is afflicted with such failings should be allowed to remain in the church without fitting reproof and ultimately exclusion, and that the true members of the church should be richly filled with many fruits of their faith. Thus the weeds will no longer cover the grain and make it unsightly, as is unfortunately often the case now, but the weeds will be covered by the grain and made inconspicuous.

Lest anyone regard this, too, as impossible, let me cite the early Christian church as an example. What was then possible cannot be absolutely impossible. Histories of the church testify that the early Christian church was in such a blessed state that as a rule Christians could be identified by their godly life, which distinguished them

---

[5] The quotations are from the King James Version of the Bible, which is closer in these instances to the German.

from other people. Tertullian wrote: "What mark do we exhibit except the prime wisdom, which teaches us not to worship the frivolous works of the human hand; the temperance, by which we abstain from other men's goods; the chastity, which we do not pollute even with a look; the compassion, which prompts us to help the needy; the truth itself, which makes us give offense; and the liberty, for which we have even learned to die? Whoever wishes to understand who the Christians are must needs employ these marks for their discovery."[6] How well things then stood! Yes, it was wonderful when dear old Ignatius could write in his letter to the Ephesians, "Those that profess themselves to be Christ's are known not only by what they say but also by what they practice."[7] It sounds magnificent when Eusebius can state in his ecclesiastical history, chapter 7, that it was as a consequence of the wicked life of the heretics that the Christian church got a bad reputation among the heathen, and then add: "But the brightness of the universal and only true church proceeded to increase in greatness, for it ever held to the same points in the same way, and radiated forth to all the race of Greeks and barbarians the reverent, sincere, and free nature, and the sobriety and purity of the divine teaching as to conduct and thought."[8] It was a great honor when the aforementioned Tertullian did not shrink from boasting in the name of the whole church before an enemy and a governor, "We never deny the deposit placed in our hands, we never pollute the marriage bed, we deal faithfully with our wards, we give aid to the needy, we render to none evil for evil."[9] Justin also records in his apology that some were converted through the uprightness and justice of the Christians in their dealings with men.[10] What beautiful praise of Christian women

[6] Tertullian, *Ad Nationes* I. iv. Spener quotes in Latin and then in German translation. Tertullian wrote his work early in the third century.
[7] Ignatius, *Epistle to the Ephesians* xiv (longer version), quoted in Greek and translated into German.
[8] Eusebius, *Ecclesiastical History* IV. vii. 3. in Greek and German.
[9] Tertullian, *To Scapula* iv, in Latin and German.
[10] Justin Martyr, *Second Apology*.

Tatian could utter when he charged the heathen with whoredom: "Among us all women are chaste"![11] So, too, Origen boasts: "The name of Jesus can produce a marvelous meekness of spirit and complete change of character, and a humanity and goodness and gentleness in those individuals who do not feign themselves to be Christians for the sake of their livelihood or the supply of any mortal wants but who have honestly accepted the doctrine concerning God and Christ and the judgment to come."[12]

On this account the early Christians were careful to examine and test the life of those who made application, and such persons were not admitted to the church until there was reason to believe that they would lead a life worthy of the calling to which they were called.[13] Origen bears witness to this in his work against Celsus.[14] Anybody who committed some offense was dealt with so severely that one must wonder how the Christians, who at that time did not have the government on their side, were able to maintain such strict discipline and order. Wrongs committed were taken up, considered, and judged by the elders of a church, over whose meetings a bishop presided. According to the case, the offenders might be excluded from the congregation and not readmitted until there was sufficient assurance of reform. Thereby the church gave evidence that it did not tolerate the sins of its members but that it deterred others from sinning and reformed those who had fallen. Moreover, it recognized as brethren only those who lived according to its standards. Justin declared, "Let those who are not found to live as Christ taught be understood to be no Christians, even though they profess with their lips the precepts of Christ." To the emperors he said expressly, "As to those who are not living according to these teachings of Christ, and are Christians only in name, we demand that

[11] Tatian, *Address to the Greeks* XXXIII. 2, in Greek and German.
[12] Origen, *Against Celsus* I. ixiii.
[13] Eph. 4:1.
[14] Origen, *op. cit.*, III. ii.

all such be punished by you."[15] In his well-known letter to Emperor Trajan the heathen Pliny himself admitted that, although he subjected some to torture in order to elicit the truth, he was unable to detect that they were guilty of any crime except their adherence to that religion which the Romans accused them of.[16] Since it is the confession of an open enemy, and that of a judge, this statement is of great weight.

If one reads the extraordinary examples of glorious virtues which have shone forth in individual Christians, one can only be deeply moved by them. What an ardent love of God it was that caused Christians to hasten toward the most horrible martyrdom rather than be terrified by it when confession of their dear Savior was at stake! How fervent was the love among themselves when they not only called one another by the endearing names of "brother" and "sister" but also lived in such a fraternal fashion that they were ready, if need be, to die for one another! If anybody wishes to read about such things, about the remarkable virtues of the early Christians and some ancient witnesses to them, I hardly know anything better to recommend than the *Christeis* of my distinguished teacher, the sainted Dr. John Conrad Dannhauer,[17] or the *Antiquitates Ecclesiae* (where such virtues are diligently recorded century by century) of my very valued friend Dr. Balthasar Bebel,[18] who was once my fellow student in Strasbourg and later my colleague.

The condition of the early Christian church puts our hot-and-cold condition to shame. At the same time it demonstrates that what we are seeking is not impossible, as many imagine. Hence it is our own fault that we are so far from deserving similar praise.

[15] Justin Martyr, *First Apology* xvi.
[16] Pliny the Younger, *Epistulae* X. 96.
[17] Johann Conrad Dannhauer, *Christeis sive Drama sacrum* (Strasbourg, 1646). Dannhauer was professor of theology in Strasbourg.
[18] Balthasar Bebel, *Antiquitates Ecclesiae in tribus prioribus post natum Christum Seculis* (Strasbourg, 1669). Bebel, 1632-1686, studied with Spener in Strasbourg and later was made professor there and in Wittenberg.

It is the same Holy Spirit who is bestowed on us by God who once effected all things in the early Christians, and he is neither less able nor less active today to accomplish the work of sanctification in us. If this does not happen, the sole reason must be that we do not allow, but rather hinder, the Holy Spirit's work. Accordingly, if conditions are improved, our discussion of this matter will not have been in vain.

I gladly acknowledge my limitations. I am not so presumptuous or conceited as to suppose that I have special insight, beyond other ministers of God, into ways of remedying the common malady. On the contrary. I daily discover faults in myself. I therefore desire from the bottom of my heart that (as some have already done) more talented men, furnished with more light, understanding, and experience, would take up this matter, ponder it in the fear of the Lord, present to the whole Evangelical church whatever they may find it necessary to suggest, and also be mindful of ways and means, by God's grace, of putting into effective use such salutary suggestions as may have been discovered. Otherwise all deliberation would be for nothing.

In a matter which concerns all of us it is incumbent on all Christians, especially all whom the Lord has set as watchmen of his church in various places, to examine the condition of the church and consider how it may be improved. This is particularly so because the church is a body which, no matter in what places it may be, has one nature. Accordingly, even if it is not always afflicted everywhere with the same diseases, it is nevertheless constantly subject to the danger of such affliction. This also means that everybody who diligently investigates and discovers what is useful to him for the improvement of his own congregation can know fairly well, without such careful observation of the somewhat different circumstances elsewhere, how other congregations may also be helped. It is beyond dispute that every preacher is called to do just this. So, after I have considered, according to the ability which God has given me, how the shortcomings of the churches which have been entrusted to me and to my dear fellow ministers may be corrected and how these churches may be built up, I make bold to set down here on paper what, on the basis of pious reflection and the guidance of the Scriptures, I think is useful and necessary. May this provide others who are more enlightened and influential in these things with an occasion to reflect further on this important matter wherever they are, to add what may be wanting in these proposals, or, if the proposals should not be practicable, to suggest better ones! I am willing to yield to anybody, no matter how simple-minded, who will show me something better and more advantageous for the discharge of my pastoral duties and whatever else has to do with edification, and I shall thank him for teaching me better. All of this is God's cause, not ours, and so he is at liberty to have such proposals made by intermediaries who are insignificant or despised in the eyes of the world but whom he has decided to bless.

Trusting in this blessing of God and willingly submitting to others who are better informed about what is best for the church, my humble opinions move in this direction, that our whole church (and the same is true of every part of it) will by God's grace be helped and will be restored to a glorious state in the following ways, among others, for I do not here mention all means (for example, the establishment of church discipline, which is of the greatest importance but which is adequately treated in the never sufficiently praised little book of discipline by the esteemed and zealous theologian John Saubert,[19] or the education of children, and the like).

---

[19] Johann Saubert, *Zuchtbüchlein der Evangelischen Kirchen* (Nürnberg, 1633).

[PART III]

[PROPOSALS TO CORRECT CONDITIONS IN THE CHURCH]

1

Thought should be given to a *more extensive use of the Word of God among us.* We know that by nature we have no good in us. If there is to be any good in us, it must be brought about by God. To this end the Word of God is the powerful means, since faith must be enkindled through the gospel, and the law provides the rules for good works and many wonderful impulses to attain them. The more at home the Word of God is among us, the more we shall bring about faith and its fruits.

It may appear that the Word of God has sufficiently free course among us inasmuch as at various places (as in this city)[1] there is daily or frequent preaching from the pulpit. When we reflect further on the matter, however, we shall find that with respect to this first proposal, more is needed. I do not at all disapprove of the preaching of sermons in which a Christian congregation is instructed by the reading and exposition of a certain text, for I myself do this. But I find that this is not enough. In the first place, we know that "all scripture is inspired by God and profitable for teaching, for reproof, for correction, and for training in righteous-

---

[1] Frankfurt am Main. Astonishing was the frequency of weekday preaching in German cities during the seventeenth century, when special preachers and series of sermons were endowed by wealthy benefactors.

ness" (II Tim. 3:16). Accordingly *all* scripture, without exception, should be known by the congregation if we are all to receive the necessary benefit. If we put together all the passages of the Bible which in the course of many years are read to a congregation in one place, they will comprise only a very small part of the Scriptures which have been given to us. The remainder is not heard by the congregation at all, or is heard only insofar as one or another verse is quoted or alluded to in sermons, without, however, offering any understanding of the entire context, which is nevertheless of the greatest importance. In the second place, the people have little opportunity to grasp the meaning of the Scriptures except on the basis of those passages which may have been expounded to them, and even less do they have opportunity to become as practiced in them as edification requires. Meanwhile, although solitary reading of the Bible at home is in itself a splendid and praiseworthy thing, it does not accomplish enough for most people.

It should therefore be considered whether the church would not be well advised to introduce the people to Scripture in still other ways than through the customary sermons on the appointed lessons.[2]

This might be done, first of all, by diligent reading of the Holy Scriptures, especially of the New Testament. It would not be difficult for every housefather to keep a Bible, or at least a New Testament, handy and read from it every day or, if he cannot read, to have somebody else read. How necessary and beneficial this would be for all Christians in every station of life was splendidly and effectively demonstrated a century ago by Andrew Hyperius,[3] whose two books on this matter were quickly translated into German by George Nigrinus[4] and, after the little work had become quite un-

---

[2] Lections of the church year.

[3] Andreas Hyperius, *De sacrae scripturae lectione ac meditatione quotidiana, omnibus omnium ordinum hominibus christianis perquam necessaria libri II* (Basel, 1561). The author, 1511-1564, was professor of theology in Marburg. The influence of Calvinism was evident in his Lutheranism.

[4] *Ein trewer und Christlicher Rath, Wie man die Heilige Schrifft teglich lesen und betrachten soll* (Mülhausen, 1562).

known, were recently brought to the attention of people again in a new edition put out by Dr. Elias Veyel,[5] my esteemed former fellow student in Strasbourg and my beloved brother in Christ.

Then a second thing would be desirable in order to encourage people to read privately, namely, that where the practice can be introduced the books of the Bible be read one after another, at specified times in the public service, without further comment (unless one wished to add brief summaries). This would be intended for the edification of all, but especially of those who cannot read at all, or cannot read easily or well, or of those who do not own a copy of the Bible.

For a third thing it would perhaps not be inexpedient (and I set this down for further and more mature reflection) to reintroduce the ancient and apostolic kind of church meetings. In addition to our customary services with preaching, other assemblies would also be held in the manner in which Paul describes them in I Corinthians 14:26-40. One person would not rise to preach (although this practice would be continued at other times), but others who have been blessed with gifts and knowledge would also speak and present their pious opinions on the proposed subject to the judgment of the rest, doing all this in such a way as to avoid disorder and strife. This might conveniently be done by having several ministers (in places where a number of them live in a town) meet together or by having several members of a congregation who have a fair knowledge of God or desire to increase their knowledge meet under the leadership of a minister, take up the Holy Scriptures, read aloud from them, and fraternally discuss each verse in order to discover its simple meaning and whatever may be useful for the edification of all. Anybody who is not satisfied with his understanding of a matter should be permitted to express his doubts and seek further explanation. On the other hand, those (including the ministers) who have made more progress should be allowed the free-

[5] The Veyel edition was published under the same title (Ulm, 1672).

dom to state how they understand each passage. Then all that has been contributed, insofar as it accords with the sense of the Holy Spirit in the Scriptures, should be carefully considered by the rest, especially by the ordained ministers, and applied to the edification of the whole meeting. Everything should be arranged with an eye to the glory of God, to the spiritual growth of the participants, and therefore also to their limitations. Any threat of meddlesomeness, quarrelsomeness, self-seeking, or something else of this sort should be guarded against and tactfully cut off especially by the preachers who retain leadership in these meetings.

Not a little benefit is to be hoped for from such an arrangement. Preachers would learn to know the members of their own congregations and their weakness or growth in doctrine and piety, and a bond of confidence would be established between preachers and people which would serve the best interests of both. At the same time the people would have a splendid opportunity to exercise their diligence with respect to the Word of God and modestly to ask their questions (which they do not always have the courage to discuss with their minister in private) and get answers to them. In a short time they would experience personal growth and would also become capable of giving better religious instruction to their children and servants at home. In the absence of such exercises, sermons which are delivered in continually flowing speech are not always fully and adequately comprehended because there is no time for reflection in between or because, when one does stop to reflect, much of what follows is missed (which does not happen in a discussion). On the other hand, private reading of the Bible or reading in the household, where nobody is present who may from time to time help point out the meaning and purpose of each verse, cannot provide the reader with a sufficient explanation of all that he would like to know. What is lacking in both of these instances (in public preaching and private reading) would be supplied by the proposed exercises. It would not be a great burden either to the preachers or to the people, and much would be done to fulfill the admonition of Paul in Colossians 3:16, "Let the word of Christ dwell in you richly, as you teach and admonish one another in all wisdom, and as you sing psalms and hymns and spiritual songs." In fact, such songs may be used in the proposed meetings for the praise of God and the inspiration of the participants.

This much is certain: the diligent use of the Word of God, which consists not only of listening to sermons but also of reading, meditating, and discussing (Ps. 1:2), must be the chief means for reforming something, whether this occurs in the proposed fashion or in some other appropriate way. The Word of God remains the seed from which all that is good in us must grow. If we succeed in getting the people to seek eagerly and diligently in the book of life for their joy, their spiritual life will be wonderfully strengthened and they will become altogether different people.

What did our sainted Luther seek more ardently than to induce the people to a diligent reading of the Scriptures? He even had some misgivings about allowing his books to be published, lest the people be made more slothful thereby in the reading of the Scriptures. His words in Volume I of the Altenburg edition of his works read:

I should gladly have seen all my books forgotten and destroyed, if only for the reason that I am afraid of the example I may give. For I see what benefit it has brought to the church that men have begun to collect many books and great libraries outside and alongside of the Holy Scriptures, and especially have begun to scramble together without any distinction, all sorts of "fathers," "councils," and "doctors." Not only has good time been wasted and the study of the Scriptures neglected, but the pure understanding of God's Word is lost. . . . It was our intention and our hope when we began to put the Bible into German that there would be less writing and more studying and reading of the Scriptures. For all other writings should point to the Scriptures. . . . Neither fathers nor councils nor we ourselves will do so well, even when our very best is done, as the

Holy Scriptures have done—that is to say, as God himself has done.
. . . I only ask in all kindness that the man who at this time wishes
to have my books will by no means let them be a hindrance to his
own study of the Scriptures, etc.[6]

Luther also wrote similar things elsewhere.[7]

One of the principal wrongs by which papal politics became en-
trenched, the people were kept in ignorance, and hence complete
control of their consciences was maintained was that the papacy
prohibited, and insofar as possible continues to prohibit, the reading of the Holy Scriptures. On the other hand, it was one of the
major purposes of the Reformation to restore to the people the
Word of God which had lain hidden under the bench (and this
Word was the most powerful means by which God blessed his
work). So this will be the principal means, now that the church
must be put in better condition, whereby the aversion to Scripture
which many have may be overcome, neglect of its study be counteracted, and ardent zeal for it awakened.

2

Our frequently mentioned Dr. Luther would suggest another
means, which is altogether compatible with the first. This second
proposal is *the establishment and diligent exercise of the spiritual
priesthood.* Nobody can read Luther's writings with some care without observing how earnestly the sainted man advocated this spiritual priesthood, according to which not only ministers but all
Christians are made priests by their Savior, are anointed by the
Holy Spirit, and are dedicated to perform spiritual-priestly acts.
Peter was not addressing preachers alone when he wrote, "You are
a chosen race, a royal priesthood, a holy nation, God's own people,
that you may declare the wonderful deeds of him who called you

[6] Luther's preface in Vol. I of the Wittenberg edition of his German works
(1539). *WA*, 50, 657, 658. English in *WML*, 1, 7-9; *LW*, 34, 283-285.
[7] Cf. *WA, Tischreden,* 4, 87, 432, 433; 5, 661, 662.

out of darkness into his marvelous light." Whoever wishes to understand and read at greater length what our Reformer's opinion on this was, and what the spiritual functions are, should read his treatise, addressed to the Bohemians, on how ministers of the church should be chosen and installed, which treatise appears in Volume II of the Altenburg edition of Luther's works.[8] There one will see how splendidly it is demonstrated that all spiritual functions are open to all Christians without exception. Although the regular and public performance of them is entrusted to ministers appointed for this purpose, the functions may be performed by others in case of emergency. Especially should those things which are unrelated to public acts be done continually by all at home and in everyday life.

Indeed, it was by a special trick of the cursed devil that things were brought to such a pass in the papacy that all these spiritual functions were assigned solely to the clergy (to whom alone the name "spiritual," which is in actual fact common to all Christians, was therefore arrogantly allotted) and the rest of the Christians were excluded from them, as if it were not proper for laymen diligently to study in the Word of the Lord, much less to instruct, admonish, chastise, and comfort their neighbors, or to do privately what pertains to the ministry publicly, inasmuch as all these things were supposed to belong only to the office of the minister. The consequence has been that the so-called laity has been made slothful in those things that ought to concern it; a terrible ignorance has resulted, and from this, in turn, a disorderly life. On the other hand, members of the so-called spiritual estate could do as they pleased since nobody dared look at their cards or raise the least objection. This presumptuous monopoly of the clergy, alongside the aforementioned prohibition of Bible reading, is one of the principal means by which papal Rome established its power over poor Christians and still preserves it wherever it has opportunity. The papacy

---

[8] *De instituendis ministris Ecclesiae ad Clarissimum Senatum Pragensem Bohemiae* (1523), in *WA*, 12, 169-196. English in *LW*, 40, 7-44.

could suffer no greater injury than having Luther point out that all Christians have been called to exercise spiritual functions (although not called to the *public* exercise of them, which requires appointment by a congregation with equal right) and that they are not only permitted but, if they wish to be Christians, are obligated to undertake them.

Every Christian is bound not only to offer himself and what he has, his prayer, thanksgiving, good works, alms, etc., but also industriously to study in the Word of the Lord, with the grace that is given him to teach others, especially those under his own roof, to chastise, exhort, convert, and edify them, to observe their life, pray for all, and insofar as possible be concerned about their salvation. If this is first pointed out to the people, they will take better care of themselves and apply themselves to whatever pertains to their own edification and that of their fellow men. On the other hand, all complacence and sloth derives from the fact that this teaching is not known and practiced. Nobody thinks this has anything to do with him. Everybody imagines that just as he was himself called to his office, business, or trade and the minister was neither called to such an occupation nor works in it, so the minister alone is called to perform spiritual acts, occupy himself with the Word of God, pray, study, teach, admonish, comfort, chastise, etc., while others should not trouble themselves with such things and, in fact, would be meddling in the minister's business if they had anything to do with them. This is not even to mention that people ought to pay attention to the minister, admonish him fraternally when he neglects something, and in general support him in all his efforts.

No damage will be done to the ministry by a proper use of this priesthood. In fact, one of the principal reasons why the ministry cannot accomplish all that it ought is that it is too weak without the help of the universal priesthood. One man is incapable of doing all that is necessary for the edification of the many persons who are generally entrusted to his pastoral care. However, if the priests do their duty, the minister, as director and oldest brother, has splendid assistance in the performance of his duties and his public and private acts, and thus his burden will not be too heavy.

More consideration ought to be given to how this whole matter, which has hardly been pursued very much since the time of Luther, may not only be made better known to the people (for which purpose the devout sermons of John Vielitz would be very useful)[9] but also be put into more extensive practice. The earlier proposal of an introductory exercise for the reading and understanding of the Scriptures should contribute not a little to this. As for me, I am very confident that if several persons in each congregation can be won for these two activities (a diligent use of the Word of God and a practice of priestly duties), together with such other things as, especially, fraternal admonition and chastisement (which have all but disappeared among us but ought to be earnestly prosecuted, and those preachers who are made to suffer in consequence should be protected as much as possible), a great deal would be gained and accomplished. Afterwards more and more would be achieved, and finally the church would be visibly reformed.

3

Connected with these two proposals is a third: the people must have impressed upon them and must accustom themselves to believing that *it is by no means enough to have knowledge of the Christian faith, for Christianity consists rather of practice.* Our dear Savior repeatedly enjoined love as the real mark of his disciples (John 13:34-35, 15:12; I John 3:10, 18, 4:7-8, 11-13, 21). In

[9] Johann Vielitz, *Regale Sacerdotium, Das ist: Die hochnötige und zugleich anmütige heilsame Lehre von dem Geist- und Königlichem Priesterthumb, in dreyen Puncten und Predigten* (Quedlinburg, 1640). This series of sermons was republished by Spener in 1671 and again in 1677, the latter edition together with Spener's own treatment of the spiritual priesthood.

his old age dear John (according to the testimony of Jerome in his letter to the Galatians)[10] was accustomed to say hardly anything more to his disciples than "Children, love one another!" His disciples and auditors finally became so annoyed at this endless repetition that they asked him why he was always saying the same thing to them. He replied, "Because it is the Lord's command, and it suffices if this be done." Indeed, love is the whole life of the man who has faith and who through his faith is saved, and his fulfillment of the laws of God consists of love.

If we can therefore awaken a fervent love among our Christians, first toward one another and then toward all men (for these two, brotherly affection and general love, must supplement each other according to II Peter 1:7), and put this love into practice, practically all that we desire will be accomplished. For all the commandments are summed up in love (Rom. 13:9). Accordingly the people are not only to be told this incessantly, and they are not only to have the excellence of neighborly love and, on the other hand, the great danger and harm in the opposing self-love pictured impressively before their eyes (which is done well in the spiritually minded John Arndt's *True Christianity*, IV, ii, 22 *et seq.*),[11] but they must also practice such love. They must become accustomed not to lose sight of any opportunity in which they can render their neighbor a service of love, and yet while performing it they must diligently search their hearts to discover whether they are acting in true love or out of other motives. If they are offended, they should especially be on their guard, not only that they refrain from all vengefulness but also that they give up some of their rights and insistence on them for fear that their hearts may betray them and feelings of hostility may become involved. In fact, they should diligently seek opportunities to do good to their enemies in order that such self-control may hurt the old Adam, who is otherwise in-

[10] Jerome, *Commentary on the Epistle to the Galatians* III. 6.
[11] Arndt, *Wahres Christenthum*, IV, ii, 22-38. English translation, pp. 474-487.

clined to vengeance, and at the same time in order that love may be more deeply implanted in their hearts.

For this purpose, as well as for the sake of Christian growth in general, it may be useful if those who have earnestly resolved to walk in the way of the Lord would enter into a confidential relationship with their confessor or some other judicious and enlightened Christian and would regularly report to him how they live, what opportunities they have had to practice Christian love, and how they have employed or neglected them. This should be done with the intention of discovering what is amiss and securing such an individual's counsel and instruction as to what ought now to be done. There should be firm resolution to follow such advice at all times unless something is expected that is quite clearly contrary to God's will. If there appears to be doubt whether or not one is obligated to do this or that out of love for one's neighbor, it is always better to incline toward doing it rather than leaving it undone.

4

Related to this is a fourth proposal: *We must beware how we conduct ourselves in religious controversies* with unbelievers and heretics. We must first take pains to strengthen and confirm ourselves, our friends, and other fellow believers in the known truth and to protect them with great care from every kind of seduction. Then we must remind ourselves of our duty toward the erring.

We owe it to the erring, first of all, to pray earnestly that the good God may enlighten them with the same light with which he blessed us, may lead them to the truth, may prepare their hearts for it or, having counteracted their dangerous errors, may reinforce what true knowledge of salvation in Christ they still have left in order that they may be saved as a brand plucked from the fire.[12] This is the meaning of the first three petitions of the Lord's Prayer,

[12] Cf. Zech. 3:2.

that God may hallow his name in them, bring his kingdom to them, and accomplish his gracious will in and for them.

2. In the second place, we must give them a good example and take the greatest pains not to offend them in any way, for this would give them a bad impression of our true teaching and hence would make their conversion more difficult.

3. In the third place, if God has given us the gifts which are needful for it and we find the opportunity to hope to win the erring, we should be glad to do what we can to point out, with a modest but firm presentation of the truth we profess, how this is based on the simplicity of Christ's teaching. At the same time we should indicate decently but forcefully how their errors conflict with the Word of God and what dangers they carry in their wake. All of this should be done in such a way that those with whom we deal can see for themselves that everything is done out of heartfelt love toward them, without carnal and unseemly feelings, and that if we ever indulge in excessive vehemence this occurs out of pure zeal for the glory of God. Especially should we beware of invectives and personal insinuations, which at once tear down all the good we have in mind to build. If we see that we have made something of a beginning in this fashion, we should be so much the more energetic in advancing what has been begun, perhaps with the assistance of others. On the other hand, if we see that they have been so captivated by their preconceived notions that, although we perceive in them a disposition to serve God gladly without being able for the present to comprehend what we have said, they are to be admonished at the very least not to slander or speak evil of the truth which they have heard from us, to reflect further on the matter in the fear of the Lord and with fervent prayer, and in the meantime to try seriously to advance in the truth and to serve their God according to the practical principles and rules of conduct which most people who call themselves Christians have to some extent in common.

To this should be added, in the fourth place, a practice of heart-felt love toward all unbelievers and heretics. While we should indicate to them that we take no pleasure in their unbelief or false belief or the practice and propagation of these, but rather are vigorously opposed to them, yet in other things which pertain to human life we should demonstrate that we consider these people to be our neighbors (as the Samaritan was represented by Christ in Luke 10:29-37 as the Jew's neighbor), regard them as our brothers according to the right of common creation and the divine love that is extended to all (though not according to regeneration), and therefore are so disposed in our hearts toward them as the command to love all others as we love ourselves demands.[13] To insult or wrong an unbeliever or heretic on account of his religion would be not only a carnal zeal but also a zeal that is calculated to hinder his conversion. A proper hatred of false religion should neither suspend nor weaken the love that is due the other person.

In the fifth place, if there is any prospect of a union of most of the confessions among Christians, the primary way of achieving it, and the one that God would bless most, would perhaps be this, that we do not stake everything on argumentation, for the present disposition of men's minds, which are filled by as much fleshly as spiritual zeal, makes disputation fruitless. It is true that defense of the truth, and hence also argumentation, which is part of it, must continue in the church together with other things instituted to build it up. Before us are the holy examples of Christ, the apostles, and their successors, who engaged in disputation—that is, vigorously refuted opposing errors and defended the truth. The Christian church would be plunged into the greatest danger if anybody wished to remove and repudiate this necessary use of the spiritual sword of the Word of God, insofar as its use against false teachings is concerned. Nevertheless, I adhere to the splendidly demonstrated assertion of our sainted Arndt in his *True Christianity*, "Purity of doctrine and

[13] Matt. 22:39.

of the Word of God is maintained not only by disputation and writing many books but also by true repentance and holiness of life."[14] The two preceding chapters are also related to this insight: "He who does not follow Christ in faith, holiness, and continued repentance cannot be delivered from the blindness of his heart but must abide in eternal darkness, nor can he have a true knowledge of Christ or fellowship with him."[15] "An unchristian life leads to false doctrine, hardness of heart, and blindness."[16]

I therefore hold (1) that not all disputation is useful and good. What our sainted Luther said holds at times: "Truth is lost not by teaching but by disputing, for disputations bring with them this evil, that men's souls are, as it were, profaned, and when they are occupied with quarrels they neglect what is most important."[17] How often the disputants themselves are persons without the Spirit and faith, filled with carnal wisdom drawn from the Scriptures, but not instructed by God! (For all knowledge which we take from the Scriptures with our own natural powers and merely human efforts, without the light of the Holy Spirit, is a carnal wisdom, else we would have to say that reason is capable of divine wisdom.) What is to be expected from such disputants? How often is unholy fire[18] brought into the sanctuary of the Lord?—that is, an unholy intent, directed not to God's glory but to man's. But such sacrifices are not pleasing to God. On the contrary, they call forth his curse, and nothing is achieved by such disputing. How often is the principle of such disputation not investigation and discovery of truth, but rather obstinate assertion of what has once been proposed, reputation for a shrewd intellect and for ingeniousness, and conquest of an opponent, no matter how this is achieved? An oppo-

[14] Arndt, *op. cit.*, I, 39. English translation, p. 132 (chapter heading).
[15] *Ibid.*, I, 37. English translation, p. 122 (chapter heading).
[16] *Ibid.*, I, 38. English translation, p. 129 (chapter heading).
[17] *WA*, 40[III], 361, "Lectures on the Psalms of Degrees" (1532-1533), on Ps. 130:5. Luther's Latin is reproduced and followed by a German rendering.
[18] Cf. Lev. 10:1.

47476

nent is so annoyed by this that, although he may not be able to answer, the manner of proceeding against him, the carnal emotions, the insults, and the like, all of which are observed and all of which savor of natural man, hinder the hoped for conversion. If one were properly to investigate the disputing which has been going on, one would find now this and now that to be at fault. One may well believe that this is the reason why all that was expected has not been achieved by this method. Disputation has in fact become so distasteful that an unseemly loathing of it has developed, and what is the fault of its abuse tends to be ascribed to disputation.

Just as all disputing is not praiseworthy and useful, so (2) proper disputation is not the only means of maintaining the truth but requires other means alongside it. Even if one resolves to limit debate to occasions in which everything is well arranged and confine it to that which is the sole and entire purpose of disputation (namely, the defense of true teaching and the refutation of the false opinions which are opposed to it in order that human reason may recognize that the former doctrine, as it is stated, conforms with the Word of God and the latter opinions do not conform), God may not add his blessing, nor will he always allow the truth to prevail. This is the case with those whose thoughts hardly extend beyond making many people Lutheran and do not deem it important that with this profession such people become genuine Christians to the very core. They therefore regard true confession of faith merely as a means of strengthening their own ecclesiastical party and not as an entrance upon a life of zealous future service of God. If the glory of God is to be properly advanced, disputation must be directed toward the goal of converting opponents and applying the truth which has been defended to a holy obedience and a due gratitude toward God. Such a *convictio intellectus* or conviction of truth is far from being faith. Faith requires more. The intention must be there to add whatever is necessary to convert the erring and remove whatever is a hindrance to him. Above all, there must be a desire, in promoting God's glory, to apply to ourselves and to all others what we hold to be true, and in this light to serve God. The glorious sayings of Christ belong here: "If any man's will is to do his will" (namely, the Father's who sent him), "he shall know whether the teaching is from God or whether I am speaking on my own authority" (John 7:17). Here our Savior says that nobody is really assured in his heart of the divine truth of his own teaching unless the will is also there to do the Father's will, and so it is not a matter merely of knowledge. "If you continue in my word, you are truly my disciples, and you will know the truth, and the truth will make you free" (John 8:31-32). "He who has my commandments and keeps them, he it is who loves me; and he who loves me will be loved by my Father, and I will love him and manifest myself to him" (John 14:21).

From all this it becomes apparent that disputing is not enough either to maintain the truth among ourselves or to impart it to the erring. The holy love of God is necessary. If only we Evangelicals would make it our serious business to offer God the fruits of his truth in fervent love, conduct ourselves in a manner worthy of our calling, and show this in recognizable and unalloyed love of our neighbors, including those who are heretics, by practicing the duties mentioned above! If only the erring, even if they cannot as yet grasp the truth which we bear witness to, would make an effort (and we ourselves should point them in this direction) to begin to serve God, in love of God and fellow man, at least to the extent of the knowledge which they may still have from Christian instruction! There is no doubt that God would then allow us to grow more and more in our knowledge of the truth, and also give us the pleasure of seeing others, whose error we now lament, alongside us in the same faith. For the Word of God has the power, if it is not viciously impeded either by those who declare it or by those who hear it, to convert men's hearts. Thus holiness of life itself contributes much to conversion, as Peter teaches (I Pet. 3:1-2).

5

Since ministers must bear the greatest burden in all these things which pertain to a reform of the church, and since their shortcomings do correspondingly great harm, it is of the utmost importance that the office of the ministry be occupied by men who, above all, are themselves true Christians and, then, have the divine wisdom to guide others carefully on the way of the Lord. It is therefore important, indeed necessary, for the reform of the church that only such persons be called who may be suited, and that nothing at all except the glory of God be kept in view during the whole procedure of calling. This would mean that all carnal schemes involving favor, friendship, gifts, and similarly unseemly things would be set aside. Not the least among the reasons for the defect in the church are the mistakes which occur in the calling of ministers, but we shall not elaborate on this here.

However, if such suitable persons are to be called to the ministry they must be available, and hence they must be trained in *our schools and universities*. May God graciously grant that everything necessary thereunto may be diligently observed by the professors of theology and that they may assist in seeing to it that the unchristian academic life, which prevails among students of all faculties and which has been sorrowfully lamented not only by the sainted and earnest John Matthew Meyfart[19] but also by many other pious persons before and after him, may by vigorous measures be suppressed and reformed. Then the schools would, as they ought, really be recognized from the outward life of the students to be nurseries of the church for all estates and as workshops of the Holy Spirit rather than as places of worldliness and indeed of the devils of ambition, tippling, carousing, and brawling.

[19] Johann Matthäus Meyfart, 1590-1642, was professor in the University of Erfurt and wrote, among other things, *Christliche Erinnerung von der Auss der Evangelischen Hochen Schulen in Teutschlandt an manchem ort entwichenen ordnungen und Erbaren Sitten, und bey dissen Elenden Zeiten eingeschlichenen Barbareyen* (1636).

The professors could themselves accomplish a great deal here by their example (indeed, without them a real reform is hardly to be hoped for) if they would conduct themselves as men who have died unto the world, in everything would seek not their own glory, gain, or pleasure but rather the glory of their God and the salvation of those entrusted to them, and would accommodate all their studies, writing of books, lessons, lectures, disputations, and other activities to this end. Then the students would have a living example according to which they might regulate their life, for we are so fashioned that examples are as effective for us as teachings, and sometimes more effective. Gregory Nazianzen declares in his panegyric on Basil that Basil's speech was like thunder because his life was like lightning *(oratio Basilii erat tonitru, quia vita ejus fulgur).*[20]

The professors should therefore exercise good discipline among those who eat at their table and not permit mischief for the sake of gain. Edifying conversation should be carried on by them at table. Unseemly talk, especially talk in which texts of the Bible, parts of hymns, and similar words are misused by twisting their meaning to evil purpose (whereby more harm is done than one may imagine, for godly persons are often disturbed in their devotions the rest of their lives whenever they come upon such words), should be averted and earnestly rebuked, not complacently tolerated.

Besides, students should unceasingly have it impressed upon them that holy life is not of less consequence than diligence and study, indeed that study without piety is worthless. The well-known saying of old Justin should always be in our minds: *Res nostrae religionis non in verbis sed in factis consistunt,* that is, the reality of our religion consists not of words but of deeds.[21] Justin learned this from St. Paul, "The kingdom of God does not consist in talk but in power" (I Cor. 4:20). Students should constantly be reminded that

[20] Gregory Nazianzen, *Carmina* 119.
[21] Justin Martyr, *Discourse to the Greeks* 35.

the rule in human life is, *Qui proficit in literis & deficit in moribus, plus deficit quam proficit,* that is, whoever grows in learning and declines in morals is on the decrease rather than the increase. This is even more valid in spiritual life, for since theology is a practical discipline,[22] everything must be directed to the practice of faith and life. The sainted Dr. John Schmidt, my dear father in Christ who served the Christian church so well, especially in Strasbourg, declared (in his *Libellus Repudii,* 2): "This is a big and terrible idol, that in higher schools and universities, even if one should be quite diligent, the mark is widely missed, for the target should be that God be glorified or, to put it more clearly, that the true and unadulterated Christian religion, the fervent practice of holiness, and Christian virtues be better planted, nurtured, and inculcated in the hearts of students."[23] What Dr. Schmidt wrote beyond this is also worth reading. At the end he calls conditions in our schools the abomination of desolation.[24]

Dr. Abraham Calovius, my especially honored patron and the theologian who is distinguished on account of the books he published with the particular purpose of defending true doctrine, briefly sums up (in his *Paedia theologica,* I, 2) the reasons why a student of theology should apply himself to holiness of life. What he writes may be translated thus:

First, because Paul so instructs his Timothy (II Tim. 2:24; I Tim. 1:18-19, 3:2, 4:7, 12; Tit. 2:7-8). Second, the Holy Spirit, who is the true and only schoolmaster, will not dwell in a heart subject to sin (John 16:12; I John 2:27). The world cannot receive the Spirit of truth (John 14:17). Third, a student of theology deals with divine wisdom, which is not carnal but spiritual and holy (James

[22] *Theologia habitus practicus est,* a common assertion of orthodoxist theologians in the seventeenth century.

[23] Johann Schmidt, *Libellus repudii oder Schrecklicher Scheid- und Absagbrieff dess eiverigen, gerechten Gottes, an alle Unbussfertige und Heuchler* (Strasbourg, 1640). Schmidt, 1594-1658, was professor of theology in Strasbourg.

[24] Cf. Matt. 24:15, King James Version.

3:15) and whose beginning is the fear of the Lord (Ps. 111:10; Prov. 1:7; 9:10). Fourth, theology does not consist merely of knowledge but also of the feelings of the heart and of practice, as we have just heard from Justin Martyr. Fifth, blessed is the man who turns words into deeds, said the ancients. "If you know these things," said Christ, "blessed are you if you do them" (John 13:17). So the disciples of Christ should search the Scriptures so as to put them into practice and do what they know. Sixth, wisdom will not enter into an evil soul and will not dwell in a body that is subject to sin (Wis. of Sol. 1:4). Whoever is addicted to sins, therefore, cannot become a dwelling place of the Holy Spirit. Seventh, as the Levites had to wash before they went into the tent of meeting (Exod. 30:18-21; I Kings 7:23-26; II Chron. 4:2-6), so those who wish to enter and leave the house of the Lord must also bestow pains on the sanctification and purification of their lives. [25]

Would to God that these words were posted before and in all lecture halls everywhere, were kept before the eyes of all students in their study rooms, and indeed were inscribed in their hearts! Then we would soon have a different church.

In this connection I cannot refrain from quoting the words of that dear and godly theologian, Dr. John Gerhard, in his harmony of the Gospels, chapter 176: "Those who are wanting in love of Christ and who neglect the practice of piety do not obtain the fuller knowledge of Christ and more abundant gift of the Holy Spirit. Hence to obtain a genuine, living, active, and salutary knowledge of divine things it is not enough to read and search the Scriptures, but it is necessary that love of Christ be added, that is, that one beware of sins against conscience, by which an obstacle is raised against the Holy Spirit, and that one earnestly cultivate piety."[26]

Surely, students of theology ought to lay this foundation, that

[25] Abraham Calov, *Paedia theologica de methodo studii theologici* (Wittenberg, 1652), pp. 57, 58. Calov, 1612-1680, professor in Wittenberg, was one of the most polemical of the orthodoxist theologians but a friend of Spener.

[26] Johann Gerhard, *Harmoniae Evangelistarum*, 1626-27 (Frankfurt, 1652), II, 2, p. 1333. Spener quotes the Latin of Gerhard and then follows with a German rendering.

during their early years of study they realize that they must die unto the world and live as individuals who are to become examples to the flock, and that this is not merely an ornament but a very necessary work, without which they may indeed be students of what may be called a philosophy of sacred things but not students of theology who are instructed and will be preserved only in the light of the Holy Spirit. Many, instead, hold that while it would be a good thing for a student of theology to lead a decent life, it is not necessary or important, provided he studies diligently and becomes a learned man, whether he allows himself to be governed by a worldly spirit during these years and participates with others in all the pleasures of the world, for there is time enough to change his manner of life when he becomes a minister—as if this were always in our power and as if a deeply ingrained love of the world did not generally cling to people throughout their lives, give them a bad reputation, and accordingly do harm to the ministry. On the other hand, if at the beginning of their study of theology all this were told to students and impressed upon them, I should hope that it would bear much fruit throughout the entire time of their study and, indeed, the rest of their lives.

It would be especially helpful if the professors would pay attention to the life as well as the studies of the students entrusted to them and would from time to time speak to those who need to be spoken to. The professors should act in such a way toward those students who, although they distinguish themselves in studying, also distinguish themselves in riotous living, tippling, bragging, and boasting of academic and other pre-eminence (who, in short, demonstrate that they live according to the world and not according to Christ) that they must perceive that because of their behavior they are looked down upon by their teachers, that their splendid talents and good academic record do not help by themselves, and that they are regarded as persons who will do harm in proportion to the gifts they receive. On the other hand, the professors should openly and expressly show those who lead a godly life, even if they are behind the others in their studies, how dear they are to their teachers and how very much they are to be preferred to the others. In fact, these students ought to be the first, or the only, ones to be promoted. The others ought to be excluded from all hope of promotion until they change their manner of life completely. This is the way it ought in all fairness to be. It is certain that a young man who fervently loves God, although adorned with limited gifts, will be more useful to the church of God with his meager talent and academic achievement than a vain and worldly fool with double doctor's degrees who is very clever but has not been taught by God. The work of the former is blessed, and he is aided by the Holy Spirit. The latter has only a carnal knowledge, with which he can easily do more harm than good.

It would not be a bad thing if all students were required to bring from their universities testimonials concerning their piety as well as their diligence and skill. Such testimonials would have to be given only after careful reflection, and never to students who do not deserve them. These measures might bring it about that students of theology would see how necessary that is to which most of them now seldom give a thought.

It would also be helpful if the professors would employ their skills to observe which studies might be useful and necessary to each student according to his intellectual gifts, his homeland, his professional goals, and the like. Some should pursue polemics with more zeal in preparation for their profession, because it is necessary that the church always have adequately equipped men to contend with enemies of the truth; rather than allowing every Goliath fearlessly to taunt the ranks of Israel, it must have some Davids who can step forward and face the Goliaths.[27] If opportunity should present itself, this matter would be helped somewhat by setting in motion the proposal which the excellent theologian, the sainted Dr.

[27] Cf. I Sam. 17.

Nicholas Hunnius, made in his *Consultatio*.[28] Other students need not make polemics their chief study, but they must also be sufficiently equipped to be able to stop the mouths of adversaries when the occasion requires and protect their congregations from error. We especially wish that those who come from lands in which there are Jews would be more diligent in learning about our controversies with these people in order that they might minister to them. On the whole, however, it would be desirable (and several excellent theologians have often expressed this wish) that disputations be held in the schools in the German language[29] so that students may learn to use the terminology which is suited to this purpose, for it will be difficult for them in the ministry when they wish to mention something about a controversy from the pulpit and must speak to the congregation in German, although they have never had any practice in this. Alongside of students who study polemics more thoroughly are others who will be adequately trained if they have a good understanding of our doctrines and know only so much of opposing doctrines as may be necessary to be secure from error and be able to show their auditors what is true and not true. When it comes to more difficult matters such men may make use of the help and advice of others.

Unless he has somebody to lead him faithfully by the hand, a beginning student will hardly know what he needs and what he does not need in these matters. For want of guidance, that will happen about which the sainted Dr. Christopher Scheibler, who wrote with good purpose, complained in the preface to his aforementioned handbook on practical theology: "If a young man devotes the whole time of his studies to controversial matters, one of

---

[28] Nikolaus Hunnius, *Consultatio, Oder Wohlmeinendes Bedencken, ob und wie die Evangelische Lutherische Kirchen die jetztschwebende Religionsstreitigkeiten entweder friedlich beylegen, oder durch Christliche und bequeme Mittel fortstellen und endigen mögen* (1632). Hunnius, 1585-1643, who was professor in Wittenberg and afterwards superintendent in Lübeck, suggested that doctrinal disputes be resolved by a commission of select men.

[29] Instead of Latin, as was then customary.

two things must be the consequence. As daily experience proves, he will either be a bungling preacher, no matter how erudite he may be in polemics, or he must become a beginner, start the study of theology all over again, and study it in a different way."[30]

In any case great care should be exercised to keep controversy within bounds. Unnecessary argumentation should rather be reduced than extended, and the whole of theology ought to be brought back to apostolic simplicity. Professors could be of great help if they not only regulated their own studies and writings accordingly but also diligently counteracted the curiosity of lustful intellects and again and again showed their antipathy to it.

It might also be useful to make more effort to put into the hands of students, and recommend to them the use of, such simple little books as the *Theologia Germanica*[31] and the writings of Tauler,[32] which, next to the Scriptures, probably made our dear Luther what he was. Such was the advice of Luther himself, who in a letter to Spalatin wrote thus of the man of God (as he called Tauler elsewhere): "If you desire to read the old, pure theology in German, you can obtain the sermons of the Dominican friar, John Tauler. Neither in the Latin nor in the German language have I found a purer, more wholesome theology or one that agrees more with the Gospel."[33] Again Luther wrote: "Once again I beg you, believe me in this case, follow me, and buy Tauler's book. I have admonished you before to get it wherever you can. You will have no trouble finding a copy. It is a book in which you will find such a skillful presentation of pure and wholesome doctrine that in

[30] Christoph Scheibler, *Manuale ad theologiam practicam* (Frankfurt, 1630).

[31] Work of an anonymous mystic, probably of the fourteenth century. English translation: *Theologia Germanica*, ed. Joseph Bernhart (New York: Pantheon Books, 1949).

[32] Although other writings have been ascribed to John Tauler, *ca.* 1300-1361, only his sermons appear to be genuine. Spener wrote an introduction to an edition of these (Frankfurt, 1681).

[33] Luther to George Spalatin, Dec. 14, 1516, in *WA, Br,* 1, 79.

comparison all other books, whether written in Greek, Latin, or Hebrew, are like iron or clay."[34] Elsewhere Luther said: "I have found more of pure, divine teaching in it than I have found or am likely to find in all the books of the scholastics in all the universities."[35] Concerning *Theologia Germanica* (which Luther also ascribed to Tauler, although it was written later, and which I look upon as a particular honor to this city inasmuch as it is supposed to have been written here in Frankfurt) Luther expressed this opinion: "To boast with my old fool,[36] no book except the Bible and St. Augustine has come to my attention from which I have learned more about God, Christ, man, and all things."[37] Hence this little book was republished and furnished with a foreword by our dear Arndt in the interest of Christian edification. Moreover, it is in order to praise him rather than criticize him that we mention that the dear man often made use of Tauler and extolled him in his *True Christianity*.[38] Thomas a Kempis' *Imitation of Christ* is to be placed beside these other two books; a few years ago it was republished for the common good together with a guide by my especially esteemed patron Dr. John Olearius,[39] who has in a praiseworthy manner promoted the practice of piety in his writings. Among older writers we should also like to mention an excellent, pious writing by an unknown author under the title *Religionis Christianae deformationis a pristino decore & desolationis causae quae, & quo pacto Christianus quisque possit ad sui conditoris reformari imaginem & amicitiam*, which is appended to the small

[34] Luther to George Spalatin, May 6, 1517, in *WA, Br*, 1, 96.

[35] "Explanations of the Disputation Concerning the Value of Indulgences" (1518), in *WA*, 1, 557; cf. English translation in *LW*, 30, 129.

[36] Cf. I Cor. 4:10.

[37] "Preface to the Complete Edition of a German Theology" (1518), in *WA*, 1, 378; cf. English translation in *LW*, 30, 75.

[38] See index in John Arndt, *True Christianity* (English translation).

[39] Thomas a Kempis, *Nachfolgung Christi* (Leipzig, 1671). Olearius, 1611-1684, was court chaplain in Halle and Weissenfels and greeted Spener's *Pia Desideria* with joy.

works of Ephraem the Syrian,[40] and many other similar writings of the ancients.

There is no doubt that such little books, to which something of the darkness of their age still clings, can and may easily be esteemed too highly, but an intelligent reader will not go astray in them. In any case, if diligently used they will accomplish much more good in students and give them a better taste of true piety than other writings which are often filled with useless subtleties and provide a good deal of easily digested fodder for the ego of the old Adam. Hopefully the reading of such books would, for many students, fulfill the ardent longing of the frequently mentioned Chytraeus, "We show ourselves to be Christians and theologians by our godly faith, holy living, and love of God and neighbors rather than by our subtle and sophistical argumentation."[41]

Just because theology is a practical discipline and does not consist only of knowledge, study alone is not enough, nor is the mere accumulation and imparting of information. Accordingly thought should be given to ways of instituting all kinds of exercises through which students may become accustomed to and experienced in those things which belong to practice and to their edification. It would be desirable if such materials were earnestly treated in certain lectures, especially if the rules of conduct which we have from our dear Savior and his apostles were impressed upon students. It would also be desirable if students were given concrete suggestions on how to institute pious meditations, how to know themselves better through self-examination, how to resist the lusts of the flesh, how to hold their desires in check and die unto the world (according to St. Augustine's rule in his *Doctrina Christiana,* chapter 7, "Men see insofar as they die unto this world, but insofar as they live unto this world they see not"),[42] how to observe growth in

---

[40] Ephraem Syrus, *Opuscula omnia* (Cologne, 1547). Ephraem was a preacher to monks in the fourth century.
[41] David Chytraeus, *Oratio de studio theologiae* (Wittenberg, 1581).
[42] Augustine, *Christian Doctrine* II. 11.

goodness or where there is still lack, and how they themselves may do what they must teach others to do. Studying alone will not accomplish this. Our dear Luther expressed this opinion (Jena ed., II, 57): "A man becomes a theologian not by comprehending, reading, or speculating but by living and indeed dying and being damned."[48]

How these exercises are to be introduced must be left to the judgment of pious and sensible professors. If I am permitted to make a suggestion, I think it would be of advantage if a godly theologian would at first take up exercises not with many students but with only those among his auditors in whom he has already observed a fervent desire to be upright Christians. With these he should undertake to treat the New Testament in such a way that, disregarding whatever has academic association, attention may be given only to what is useful for their edification. This should be done in such fashion that each student may be permitted to say what he thinks about each verse and how he finds that it applies to his own and to others' benefit. The professor, as the leader, should reinforce good observations. If he sees, however, that students are departing from the end in view, he should proceed in clear and friendly fashion to set them right on the basis of the text and show them what opportunity they have to put this or that rule of conduct into practice. Such confidence and friendship should be established among the students that they not only admonish one another to put what they have heard into practice but also inquire, each for himself, where they may have failed to observe the rules of conduct and try at once to put them into practice. They should also come to a mutual agreement to keep an eye on one another and, with brotherly admonitions suitable thereto, see how one or another may accommodate himself. In fact, they ought to give an account to one another and to their professor of how, in this or

[48] Luther, "Operationes in Psalmos" (1519-1521), commenting on Ps. 5:12, in *WA*, 5, 163.

that situation, they have acquitted themselves in the light of the given rules.

In such a confidential relationship in which every matter that concerns the participants (for they must quickly learn not to make rash judgments about others or pass sentence on anyone outside the group) is examined according to the Word of God, it should soon become evident how far one has progressed and where in particular there may still be need for help. The professor would exercise no other authority over the consciences given into his care than, as one who is more experienced, to point out, on the basis of the sole authority of the Word of God, what his opinion in any given case may be; and as the students become more and more experienced the professor should be able to confer with them as colleagues. If this practice were continued for a while with fervent and earnest prayers to God, and each person, especially when he wished to prepare himself for the Lord's Supper, were to describe the condition of his conscience to the whole group[44] and were always to act according to its counsel, I have no doubt that within a short time a glorious advance in piety would result. If the proposal really got into motion, more and more would be attracted, to their advantage, and finally the participants could become young men who are upright Christians (before they enter the ministry, where they should make others Christians) and who take pains to *do* rather than to *teach*. This is what real teachers in the school of our Savior ought to be. My valued friend and dear brother in the Lord, Mr. Gottlieb Spitzel, who probably bears the ruin of Joseph[45] inwardly in his heart, describes this with pleasing and worthy examples in his *Vetus Academia Jesu Christi.*[46] His *Pius literati hominis secessus,*[47] also an uncommonly useful work, can provide light and support

[44] *Collegium.* The *collegium pietatis* was a group or meeting for the cultivation of personal holiness.
[45] Cf. Amos 6:6.
[46] Gottlieb Spitzel, "Old School of Jesus Christ" (Augsburg, 1671).
[47] Gottlieb Spitzel, "Pious Retreat of the Learned Man" (Augsburg, 1669).

for the design of preparing godly theologians and can be read with profit by all students who embark on their studies with the right purpose.

6

In addition to these exercises, which are intended to develop the Christian life of the students, it would also be useful if the teachers made provision for practice in those things with which the students will have to deal when they are in the ministry. For example, there should be practice at times in instructing the ignorant, in comforting the sick, and especially in preaching, where it should be pointed out to students that everything in their sermons should have edification as the goal. I therefore add this as a sixth proposal whereby the Christian church may be helped to a better condition: that *sermons* be so prepared by all that their purpose (faith and its fruits) may be achieved in the hearers to the greatest possible degree.

There are probably few places in our church in which there is such want that not enough sermons are preached.[48] But many godly persons find that not a little is wanting in many sermons. There are preachers who fill most of their sermons with things that give the impression that the preachers are learned men, although the hearers understand nothing of this. Often many foreign languages are quoted, although probably not one person in the church understands a word of them. Many preachers are more concerned to have the introduction shape up well and the transitions be effective, to have an outline that is artful and yet sufficiently concealed, and to have all the parts handled precisely according to the rules of oratory and suitably embellished, than they are concerned that the materials be chosen and by God's grace be developed in such a way that the hearers may profit from the sermon in life and death. This

[48] See above, p. 87, n. 1.

ought not to be so. The pulpit is not the place for an ostentatious display of one's skill. It is rather the place to preach the Word of the Lord plainly but powerfully. Preaching should be the divine means to save the people, and so it is proper that everything be directed to this end. Ordinary people, who make up the largest part of a congregation, are always to be kept in view more than the few learned people, insofar as such are present at all.

As the Catechism[49] contains the primary rudiments of Christianity, and all people have originally learned their faith from it, so it should continue to be used even more diligently (according to its meaning rather than its words) in the instruction of children,[50] and also of adults if one can have these in attendance. A preacher should not grow weary of this. In fact, if he has opportunity, he would do well to tell the people again and again in his sermons what they once learned, and he should not be ashamed of so doing.

I shall here gladly pass over additional observations that might well be made about sermons, but I regard this as the principal thing: Our whole Christian religion consists of the inner man or the new man, whose soul is faith and whose expressions are the fruits of life, and all sermons should be aimed at this. On the one hand, the precious benefactions of God, which are directed toward this inner man, should be presented in such a way that faith, and hence the inner man, may ever be strengthened more and more. On the other hand, works should be so set in motion that we may by no means be content merely to have the people refrain from outward vices and practice outward virtues and thus be concerned only with the outward man, which the ethics of the heathen can also accomplish, but that we lay the right foundation in the heart, show that what does not proceed from this foundation is mere hypocrisy, and hence accustom the people first to work on what is

---

[49] Luther's *Small Catechism* (1529) with accompanying instruction.
[50] *Kinderlehre*, public instruction in the Catechism for children, and sometimes adults as well, often held on Sunday afternoons.

inward (awaken love of God and neighbor through suitable means) and only then to act accordingly.

One should therefore emphasize that the divine means of Word and sacrament are concerned with the inner man. Hence it is not enough that we hear the Word with our outward ear, but we must let it penetrate to our heart, so that we may hear the Holy Spirit speak there, that is, with vibrant emotion and comfort feel the sealing of the Spirit[51] and the power of the Word. Nor is it enough to be baptized, but the inner man, where we have put on Christ in Baptism,[52] must also keep Christ on and bear witness to him in our outward life. Nor is it enough to have received the Lord's Supper externally, but the inner man must truly be fed with that blessed food. Nor is it enough to pray outwardly with our mouth, but true prayer, and the best prayer, occurs in the inner man, and it either breaks forth in words or remains in the soul, yet God will find and hit upon it. Nor, again, is it enough to worship God in an external temple, but the inner man worships God best in his own temple,[53] whether or not he is in an external temple at the time. So one could go on.

Since the real power of all Christianity consists of this, it would be proper if sermons, on the whole, were pointed in such a direction. If this were to happen, much more edification would surely result than is presently the case. We have a glorious example of this in the postil of the precious, gifted, and sainted John Arndt to which these lines are a preface. Just as this excellent preacher and disciple of Luther (who was the model for most of John Arndt's modes of expression, including some which have been misunderstood and hence misinterpreted) made everything in his other spiritual writings turn on the real core, the inner man, so he has a similar object in his postil, which is here presented to the church

[51] Cf. Eph. 1:14; 4:30.
[52] Cf. Gal. 3:27.
[53] Cf. I Cor. 3:16.

in a new and complete edition. His auditors were wonderfully edified by these sermons during his lifetime, and since then many thousands of godly souls have felt strongly the power of his method and blessed work, have humbly thanked God for his precious gifts, and have kept alive the memory of this dear author. The frequent editions of his postil, all of which have been exhausted, and the increasing demand for it, among other things testify to the benefits derived from this glorious book. This shows that this work, unlike others, is not of the kind that dies with its author or ceases to please after its first eager reading because its novelty has worn off. Neither the author nor this (or any other) writing of his requires my praise. I am not the one through whose testimony his reputation can be increased, for I count it an honor and gain to pay homage to him as one of his disciples. Nevertheless, I am certain that if all our teaching, writing, and preaching were patterned after John Arndt's, it would not be necessary to express so many complaints as we are now often justified in expressing.

I prefer to leave to every reader's own feeling and experience what I might otherwise (if I were to do it) have to say in praise of this work. I shall now proceed simply to indicate to the Christian reader what has actually been done to make this new edition helpful to him as he uses it. The following are to be noted:

(1) The former Merian edition,[54] which has served as the basis for the present new edition, has been discussed with others and examined carefully, its mistakes (which were found here and there) were corrected, and what was missing in it was supplied. Retained and to be found here, therefore, are the improvements of former editions mentioned in the preface to the Merian edition, such as the translation of Latin quotations, the completion of biblical verses and texts which were briefly indicated, etc.

(2) The Lenten sermons, which were printed in various places, have been brought together in the hope of making them more ac-

[54] Published in Frankfurt by Matthäus Merian, Jr., 1621-1687.

cessible to the reader. The same thing has been done with other sermons found in the appendix. These have been incorporated under the festivals or other places in which they are appropriate. A comparison of the index of sermons with the former index will show this.

(3) The printing has been so planned that, although there is more text in this edition and the type is not less readable, the bulk has been reduced considerably in order to get everything into one volume.

(4) Not only have the verse references been inserted alongside the chapter references in biblical citations, but almost countless passages which the sainted author alluded to but whose chapters and verses were not indicated have been printed in full for the great benefit of the reader. All of this was promised but not done in the former Merian edition.

(5) We have wished to append Arndt's explanation of the Catechism[55] to the deeply spiritual work of this dear man on the Psalms.[56] On the other hand, his *True Christianity* as well as his little book of doctrine and comfort,[57] his doctrine of union with Christ,[58] and his repetition and defense of the teaching of *True Christianity*[59] have only recently been published again. Moreover, his *Garden of Paradise*[60] is often encountered in all sorts of places. Our aim has been to incorporate in the present volume whatever else of this glorious man does not appear in these other works in order that all remaining crumbs might be preserved.

---

[55] *Der gantze kleinere Catechismus des grossen Lutheri sel.*

[56] *Der gantze Psalter Davids, des h. Königs und Propheten, in 462 Predigten aussgelegt und erklärt.*

[57] *Lehr und Trost-büchlein, vom Glauben und heiligen Leben, zum wahren Christenthumb gehörig.*

[58] *Von der Vereinigung der Gleubigen mit Christo Jesu ihrem Haupt.*

[59] *Repetitio Apologetica, oder Wiederholung und Verantwortung der Lehre vom wahren Christenthumb.*

[60] *Paradiess-Gärtlein.* There is an anonymous English translation, *Garden of Paradise* (London, 1716).

Nothing else was found after diligent search than some sermons delivered at the accession of a ruler and the opening of a session of the diet[61] and his suggested inscriptions for gift Bibles.[62] These have on this account been published here with the rest, although the last item is believed by some not to be the sainted Arndt's work but that of one of his admirers.

(6) In any book a well-made index is not only a splendid ornament (a man told his good friend, a prominent theologian, whose books were furnished with no indexes or, at best, poor indexes, that he was reminded by these of an otherwise well-adorned maiden who forgot to put on a garland) but also an excellent help to relocate (if need be) a passage which has been read and to apply everything to better purpose. Accordingly three indexes have been added to this edition: an index of sermons, an index of biblical texts, and an index of noteworthy subjects. What was lacking in all previous editions has thus been supplied in the present one.

Since all this has been carefully planned and no pains or costs have been spared, I have no doubt that the Christian reader will have abundant pleasure in the present edition and that in his use of it he will be able, with God's grace, to edify himself magnificently. I do not propose to add anything more to this report about our new edition. As I have indicated above, I prefer to leave to the reader's own experience and judgment what sort of profit he may find in this book in its present form.

At the same time I earnestly admonish the reader not to jump to hasty conclusions if he should at times find, in this and other works of the beloved author, some expressions or teachings which at first sight may seem strange to him. He should thoroughly ponder their true meaning and employ fervent prayer. I have

---

[61] *Eine Huldigungs Predigt . . . . Auch eine Landtages Predigt.*
[62] *Informatorium biblicum: Das ist, Etzliche christliche Erinnerungs-Puncten, so als ein Denckmahl im eingang einer Bibel sollen geschrieben werden.*

no doubt that he will himself discover that everything is in accord with the Scriptures and the method of teaching prescribed for us there and that it is far removed from all heresy. On the contrary, it is directed toward an honest cultivation of true orthodoxy (not the vain reputation of an orthodoxy that consists merely of doctrinal statements but a living knowledge of effective Christianity) and what such orthodoxy is aimed at, namely, the inner man. In this connection I cannot sufficiently recommend to the diligent reader of *True Christianity* and other books of Arndt the profitable use of the defense of *True Christianity* by the sainted Henry Varenius,[63] who has rendered true piety a service in his book. The reader will here recognize how much that is impressive and edifying lies in those passages, when properly examined, which have been misunderstood by others. I wish that Varenius' book would be reprinted and become better known, or (in order not to give the impression that it is the intention to revive old controversies) that a sufficiently informed person would abridge and publish only the explanations which pertain to the defense and proper understanding of Arndt.

In conclusion, I call fervently on the gracious God and giver of all good things that, as he has once allowed many good seeds of his Word to be scattered abroad through his faithful servant who has long since entered into his peace, and as he has hitherto powerfully blessed many of these grains that fell into godly hearts and bore not a little fruit (for which thanks be to God forever!), so he may continue to give his blessing to the book which is still extant and is now prepared for wider use in this edition, that many who with devout and simple hearts seek their edification on Sundays in these sermons as well as in the Holy Scriptures may also abundantly find it here and return to God their fruits of thanks-

---

[63] Heinrich Varenius, *Christliche, Schrifftmässige, wohlgegründete Rettung der vier Bücher vom wahren Christenthum* (2nd ed.; Lüneburg, 1689).

giving.⁶⁴ May many preachers themselves be revived thereby to preach the heart of Christianity after this model with simplicity and power. In general, may it also be a means for some further reform of the wretched condition of our church which we deplored so heartily above. Everything, however, be to the glory of God himself and (which has the same outcome) the advance of his kingdom for the sake of Jesus Christ. Amen.

Frankfurt am Main
March 24, 1675

PHILIP JACOB SPENER, TH.D.,
pastor and senior of the
ministerium in Frankfurt

---

⁶⁴ Cf. Heb. 13:15, King James Version.

TABLE OF CONTENTS OF THE
APPENDIXES[1]

First Christian Comment

Shortcomings in the civil authorities; in the clergy. Ignorance of true Christianity. Controversies. Desire for ecumenical standards of doctrine to oppose all sects. Observance of Christian love in the writings and judgments of fellow believers. Philosophy. Exercises in universities. High cost of books. Shortcomings in the home. First Epistle of John on the evidences of love in Christians. Of death-bed repentance. Drunkenness. Lawsuits. Faults of judges; of lawyers; of magistrates; of parties.

Business procedures today. Certain rules of business. Especially concerning purchases. Commissions. Whether damage is to be charged to the wares. Sales. Godliness a means of blessing. Other virtues. Inns. The duty of innkeepers. Artisans. Husbandmen and farmers. Community of goods. Beggars. How to prevent them. The faith of the masses a deception of the devil. Measures against this. Other vain delusions. Offense of the heathen; of the papists. How these are recognized.

Whether or not there is hope for better conditions in the church. Whether godly people desire a papal compulsion of conscience. What we think of good works and how we promote them. Whether inborn weakness may be pleaded as an excuse. Whether

---

[1] The two comments on the *Pia Desideria* which Spener solicited (see above, pp. 16, 17) and published as appendixes are considerably longer than Spener's own work. Their contents are reflected in the table of contents which is here reproduced. The final supplement on the conversion of the Jews and the fall of Rome is by Spener.

people are driven to despair by the teaching of true faith. Whether one should preach differently on account of pretended offense. What is required in the way of perfection. That we are obligated to reflect on the reform of the church. And really put our hands to the task. How the weak may be assisted by a community of goods. What kind of instrument church discipline is.

Education of youth. How the damage is to be corrected. How young people may be given more help in their studies and trades. *Collegia pietatis* in schools. Scriptures as the handbook of the principles of true Christianity. How learning is to be set in motion. Preliminary exercises of students of theology. Practice in preaching. Further acceleration of the reform of conduct among students of theology. Testimonials and recommendations of students. False inflation of theologians. Academic degrees and their abuse.

Arrangement to lead people to the way of the Lord. Treatment of controversies in sermons. Promotion of reform in conduct. Private conversation of ministers. Scrutiny. Treatment of the Scriptures. Public reading. Whether the apostolic sort of church meetings would be useful, and certain warnings in connection therewith. Spiritual priesthood. Whether auditors are to speak to and censure their preachers. Practice of the spiritual priesthood among theologians themselves; among dependents and others. It is not enough to promote knowledge, for practice also belongs to Christianity. The confessor's procedure with the confessant. Communion of the sick. Temptation to believers from unbelievers. Whether there is hope for the reform of the latter. How this may be attempted. Establishment of friendship among the godly. Exclusion of self-glory. Prayer. That every preacher take hold in his sermons of the work in his community. Need for this. Dealing with individuals. Godly walk of preachers, and their avoidance of the appearance of evil. Also of subordinate ministers, and how this may be accomplished. Other remedies.

Correspondence with foreigners about the work of the Lord.

Also with civil rulers and persons in high and noble station. Necessary help from civil authorities. The writing of books. Greetings of peace to others. Travel of theologians to foreign lands. Conclusion.

Second Christian Comment

About the preface in general. Complaint about wretched conditions in the church. More crafty persecution: caesaropapism and corrupt ministry. Unknown abominations. Christian community of goods. Obscure belief. Offense of unbelief and heresy. Weak Nicodemuses, Anabaptists. Right to reproach such errors. Whether a conversion of the Jews is to be expected. Or a greater collapse of the papacy. The possibility of achieving a measure of perfection. Useful to introduce the apostolic method of teaching. Reading of the Scriptures. Departure from its proper meaning. How everything in the Scriptures is to be carefully examined for certainty. Royal priesthood. Anabaptists. Religious controversy and the protection of believers. Why the unbelieving are hard to convert. One must proceed against opponents as far as they themselves go. One should not find fault with the professors for the subtleties which are called forth in their polemical writings. Lack of discipline in children an impediment to professors. How this may be corrected. Selection of authors for reading. Tauler, Kempis, etc. *Collegium pietatis.*

Supplement

Which theologians have taught that the conversion of the Jews is to be expected. In the ancient church. In our Evangelical church. Which of our theologians maintains that a fall of Babel is to be expected. Papists who anticipate the destruction of Rome.

INDEX

INDEX

Absolution, 65, 67
Affelmann, John, 50
Aland, Kurt, 17, 28
Andreae, John Valentine, 6, 54
Aristotle, 6, 25
Arndt, John, 8, 15-17, 27, 31, 33,
  66, 96, 99, 100, 111, 117, 119,
  121
Augustine, 111, 112

Babel, Babylon, 39, 40, 69, 71-
  73, 125; see also Papacy
Baptism, 63, 65, 66, 117
Basil, 104
Baxter, Richard, 2, 9
Bayly, Lewis, 9, 10, 14, 17
Bebel, Balthasar, 84
Bernard of Clairvaux, 50
Bunyan, John, 1

Caesaropapism, 44, 125
Calixtus, George, 13
Calovius, Abraham, 18, 105
Canstein, Carl Hildebrand von, 9
Catechism, 63, 116
Chrysostom, 44
Church, 67, 85; union of, 99
Chytraeus, David, 50, 52, 112
Classes, social, 4, 5, 42
Clericalism, 43, 44

Collegia pietatis, 13, 14, 19, 20,
  89-91, 113, 114, 125
Community of goods, 60-62
Consistory, 3, 4
Controversy, 5-7, 19, 26, 87-102,
  108, 123, 125
Conversion, 76, 80, 125
Council, 32

Dancing, 2, 10, 22, 23
Dannhauer, Jonh Conrad, 10, 17,
  84
Dinckel, John, 53
Discipline, 83, 104
Donatism, 20
Dorsch, John George, 68
Dorsche, John 35
Dort, Synod of, 26
Drunkenness, 2, 10, 21, 22, 58,
  59, 107, 123
Dury, John, 12
Dyke, Daniel, 9

Ephraem, 112
Eusebius, 39, 82

Faith, 64, 124
Francke, August Herman, 21, 22

Gerhard, John, 6, 7, 17, 48. 106

Gregory Nazianzen, 49, 104
Grossgebauer, Theophilus, 6

Hartmann, John Lewis, 48
Hasidism, 1
Helwig, Jacob, 68
Hochburg, Christian, 45
Horb, John Henry, 16, 17, 22, 34
Hunnius, Nicholas, 109
Hyperius, Andrew, 88

Ignatius, 82

Jansenism, 1
Jerome, 96
Jews, 15, 17, 68, 69, 72, 76-79, 109, 125
Judgment, last, 36
Julian the Apostate, 41
Justin Martyr, 82, 84, 104, 106

Kempis, Thomas a, 17, 11, 125
Knowledge vs. practice, 95-97
Korthold, Christian, 41

Labadie, Jean de, 11, 14, 17
Laity, 13, 19, 20, 57, 92-95
Latin, 5, 7, 10, 118
Lawsuits, 59, 123
Leibniz, Gottfried Wilhelm, 12
Life, Christian, 95-97
Lord's Supper, 7, 20, 24, 26, 63, 65-67, 114, 117, 124
Love, 96, 97, 99, 102, 106
Luetkemann, Joachim, 14
Luther, Martin, 10, 40, 51-53, 58, 63-65, 69, 76-78, 91, 93-95, 100, 110, 111, 113

Mayer, John Frederick, 22
Meisner, Balthasar, 6, 47
Menzel, Jerome, 52

Meyfart, John Matthew, 103
Ministers, 32, 44-57, 93, 94
Muhlenberg, Henry Melchior, 22
Mysticism, 8, 19, 27

Nigrinus, George, 88

Olearius, John, 111
Opus operatum, 65, 67
Origen, 83
Orthodoxy, Eastern, 39

Papacy, Pope, 41, 42, 77, 93, 123; see also Babel; Roman Catholic
Pascal, Blaise, 1
Perfection, 19, 81, 124, 125
Persecution, 41, 42
Pliny, 84
Polemics; see Controversy
Polycarp, 39
Praetorius, Stephen, 45
Prayer, 117
Preaching, 63, 65, 66, 87, 91, 115-122
Priesthood, spiritual, 19, 20, 92-95, 124
Professors, 104, 107, 108, 110, 113
Puritan, 1, 9, 14

Quaker, 23, 47

Raith, Balthasar, 54
Reason, 56, 100
Roman Catholic, 5, 40, 47, 49, 69, 70, 75, 77; see also Babel
Rosicrucian, 23, 48
Rufinus, 41
Rulers, 3-5, 7, 43, 60, 79, 125

Sarcerius, Erasmus, 78
Saubert, John, 86

Scheibler, Christopher, 49, 109, 110

Schleiermacher, F. D., 27

Schmidt, John, 105

Schools, 103-115, 123

Scriptures, 25, 46, 51, 56, 87-92, 114, 124, 125

Selnecker, Nicholas, 53

Senior, 4, 12, 33

Service of God, 62

Sontham, Emanuel, 9

Spener, Philip Jacob: early life, 8-11; travel, 11; activity in Frankfurt, 11-14; *Pia Desideria*, 14-20, 31-35; activity in Dresden, 21-22; in Berlin, 22-24; estimate of, 24-28

Spitzel, Gottlieb, 114

Stoll, Joachim, 8, 11, 16, 34

Students, 104

Sunday, 10, 11, 12

Superintendent, 4

Tarnov, Paul, 62

Tauler, John, 17, 27, 110, 111, 125

Teelinck, Willem, 1

Tennent, Gilbert, 1

Tertullian, 82

Theater, 22, 23

Theologia Germanica, 110, 111

Trajan, Emperor, 84

Varenius, Henry, 50, 121

Veyel, Elias, 89

Vielitz, John, 95

Weigel, Valentine, 47

Weigelian, 47, 48

Weller, Jacob, 54

Wesley, John, 1, 24

Word of God, 87, 102, 117

Works, good, 63

Zeller, Christopher, 54

Zesch, William, 69

Zinzendorf, Nicholas, 1, 24

Zunner, John David, 31

Type: Body, 11 on 13 and 10 on 11 Garamond
Display, Garamond
Paper: 'R' Antique

SEMINAR EDITIONS

Philip Jacob Spener, *Pia Desideria.* Translated, edited, and with an Introduction by Theodore G. Tappert.

Martin Kähler, *The So-Called Historical Jesus and the Historic, Biblical Christ.* Translated, edited, and with an Introduction by Carl E. Braaten.

Samuel Simon Schmucker, *Fraternal Appeal to the American Churches, with a Plan for Catholic Union on Apostolic Principles.* Edited and with an Introduction by Frederick K. Wentz.

Vilhelm Beck, *Memoirs.* A Story of Renewal in the Denmark of Kierkegaard and Grundtvig. Edited and with an Introduction by Paul C. Nyholm. Translated by C. A. Stub.

Nathan Söderblom, *The Nature of Revelation.* Translated by Frederic E. Pamp. Edited and with an Introduction by Edgar M. Carlson.

Eric Norelius, *The Journals of Eric Norelius: A Swedish Missionary on the American Frontier.* Translated, edited, and with an Introduction by G. Everett Arden.

Others in preparation.

622-1
5-39